Why Not Us?

Why Not Us?

❖

The 86-Year Journey
of the Boston Red Sox Fans
from Unparalleled Suffering
to the Promised Land
of the 2004 World Series

❖

Leigh Montville

PublicAffairs

NEW YORK

For

LEIGH BLISS MONTVILLE (1900–1967)

BOOK DESIGN AND COMPOSITION BY JENNY DOSSIN

ISBN 1-58648-333-1

First Edition

1 3 5 7 9 10 8 6 4 2

Contents

Q: Why do you keep hitting your head on that wall?
A: Because it will feel so good when I stop.

—*Oldest Joke in the World*

Why Not Us?

1. The Story

L ET US BEGIN WITH KAY-KAY CLIVIO. SHE IS IN INDIA, for goodness' sake, climbing a mountain. This is the middle of the summer of 2004. How is the weather, Kay-Kay? Is it hot?

"It's India!" she says. "It's like a million degrees."

She is living in a city called Mysore, having traveled all the way from Charlestown, Massachusetts, to study at the Ashtanga Yoga Research Institute for a month. She is heading to the top of this mountain, Chamundi Hill, about 1,000 steps to climb at the start, then a two-mile walk, to see a guru and talk about the Boston Red Sox and their cursed existence.

She is halfway around the world, but she is wearing her Boston Red Sox cap and has just gone to a cyber café to check on last night's result from Fenway Park in the web pages of the *Boston Globe*. Crazy place, this India. Can't find a cheeseburger, but you can read about the Red Sox in the *Boston Globe*.

The New York Yankees fans at the Institute—can't find a cheeseburger, but there are Yankees fans—have been giv-ing her the normal amount of grief that Yankees fans always give people from Boston. She has responded by finding out about this guru who can exercise a puja, very powerful medicine, and remove curses and bad luck and maybe acne for a specified price.

The only problem—here's the guru now—is that he doesn't speak. He is a silent guru. Kay-Kay is beside herself. She is telling him about all the bad things, you know, starting back in 1918 and going all the way to 2003 and Aaron Boone, home run, bottom of the 11th. Do you know about Bill Buckner? The guru doesn't blink. He seems confused. He not only doesn't speak but doesn't seem to understand English and certainly knows nothing about baseball.

Disappointed, Kay-Kay and her friend walk back down the mountain and head toward the Institute when they spot a place where palms are read. What could this be? They step inside and find an old man sitting near an altar. Why an altar? The old man says he can take care of problems (for an offering). He can cure ailments from arthritis to broken hearts. He can do black magic if desired.

Why not? She goes into the tale of 86 years of misery—"Don't talk to me about 1986; I'm from a family of seven kids, four boys, and they were all crying around the table in Medford and I was ten years old and never had seen one of my brothers cry"—and the old man starts burning things and saying some words over a very large bone.

"It looks like a human femur bone," Kay-Kay reports.

The old man stops. The ceremony is done. The old man asks for 20,000 rupees.

"Not so fast," Kay-Kay replies, because she is from Charlestown, Massachusetts, and wasn't born the day after yesterday. "I'll give you 15,000. The other 5,000, I'll get to you when I see some results. Okay?"

So what to do now that the silly thing worked?

Kay-Kay Clivio, owner of Charlestown Yoga, has to come up with the 5,000 rupees. She can't find the old man's card and may have to go all the way back to India. A debt is a debt. The femur bone worked.

"My sister says I should take all the credit," Kay-Kay says, home again, a couple of months later, the Boston Red Sox the champions of the baseball world. "I don't see it that way. I think everyone gets credit. I think everyone has been doing things for all these years. How many little kids prayed every night? How many old people lit candles? I think it just all added up. We all played a part. We all did it. We were just overwhelming in the end. We overcame the negative energy."

The stories are the story. Are they not? The headlines and hosannahs and the ticker-tape parades are for the players and management, the doers of the deed, outlasting the accursed Yankees in seven games, finishing off the St. Louis Cardinals in a four-game sweep to win the World Series at twenty minutes until midnight on October 27, 2004, but this time the people in the crowd are more important than the people in the procession.

Eighty-six years. Eighty-six years. Eighty-six years. There never has been a story in American sport that came close to the long march to a baseball championship in

Boston from 1918 until that final out at Busch Stadium in St. Louis. Generations came and generations went, and there never was a celebration. Until now.

Who felt better at the end, the players or the people? Who? The end was stepping out the front door in Stalingrad the morning after the Germans had departed the city limits. Liberation. The air smelled different. The light seemed to come from a new direction.

"I watched the final game wearing my father's Red Sox hat," Marty Carney of Roslindale says. "I put his picture on the table, right next to the ten beers. I thought about him the whole game. He had season tickets for about fifty years. The day after the Red Sox won, I went to the cemetery. The ground was all messed up. It was from him spinning in his grave."

How many trips were made to how many cemeteries? How many old, old, very old bottles of champagne finally were opened? To have watched the Red Sox was to have been wrapped up in a saga, one of those 900-page potboilers that never end, every chapter closing with a damsel in distress or a dropped pop-up to third base. Would it ever be done? Finished? Ever?

"I went to the cemetery to see Poppa, my grandfather," Joe Zimmer of Milton says. "I bought one of those World Championship pennants to put on his grave. I said my prayer, looked up. There were pennants all over the place on graves."

The players were wonderful—the redoubtable Curt Schilling, the smiling David Ortiz, the mercurial Manny Ramirez, the good-looking Johnny Damon, the ever-dancing Pedro Martinez, all of them—but they were no more than mechanics, plumbers and electricians brought in to finally do the job right. For all of their many heroics—and there were a lot of heroics—they were imported workmen on what had been a continually botched endeavor. They didn't live in that house. They didn't eat, sleep, watch cable television there day in and day out. They didn't know its history.

The people in the house had lived with disappointment so long it was a gray wallpaper, a background to daily existence. The pipes clanged, fuses burned out, the rabbit ears always needed adjustment. The Red Sox . . . oh well. Things happen.

There seemed to be a calamity in history for every age group. Granddad could talk about '46 and Ted Williams going 5-for-25 in the World Series, Enos Slaughter of the St. Louis Cardinals scoring all the way from first in the seventh and final game while the relay came from center fielder Leon Culberson to shortstop Johnny Pesky and then too late at home. Or '48 and that one-game playoff against the Cleveland Indians. Denny Galehouse! Or '49, two games to play in New York against the Yankees to end the season, win one and the pennant is clinched. Dad could talk about '67, the Impossible Dream that came up short in seven games, again against the Cards. Or maybe '75, seven games, a sad finish after Carlton Fisk's dramatic home run against the Cincinnati Reds in the sixth. Or '78 and Bucky Dent. Oh no, Bucky Dent.

The older kids had 1986 to think about, sixth game, New York Mets, Shea Stadium, one out away, then Mookie Wilson hits that ground ball to Bill Buckner at first. The youngest kids, young as one year old, could look back to 2003, seventh game at Yankee Stadium. Tim Wakefield throws a knuckleball to start the bottom of the 11th inning in the seventh game at Yankee Stadium. Aaron Boone swings. Enough said.

The rigors of handling any or all of this—and no matter your age, you soon were handed the entire history, almost as if your Armenian grandmother were describing long-ago life with the Turks—became almost comical. Jokes were easy. Punch lines, alas, always were at the speaker's expense.

"I came home from St. Lawrence Grammar School and listened to the final game of the 1946 World Series," Ed Leavitt, an attorney from West Haven, Connecticut, says. "I was on my knees in my bedroom, praying the Rosary. Enos Slaughter came around from first, and it was the first time I ever questioned God."

"My wife was pregnant during the 1986 World Series," Geoff Hobson, born in Framingham, remembers. "I read somewhere that it was beneficial to talk to the baby in the womb. I would get down close to my wife's stomach every night and tell the baby about the Red Sox and the Series. I talked about history, especially about Carl Yastrzemski. I love Yaz. I talked about the games.

"The only problem was that I stopped after game five. I couldn't tell him what happened next. It was all too sad. The way I left it with my son in the womb, the Red Sox are still up three games to two."

Who couldn't laugh at the weird turns of fate?

"I was working for the *Globe* for game six at Shea Stadium in 1986," Ian Thomsen, now a senior writer for *Sports Illustrated*, says. "Midway through the game, the Red Sox leading, my boss, Vince Doria, gave me my assignment. He said, 'Write a story about how John McNamara, the Red Sox manager, is a genius. He's made some wonderful moves. He's brought the World Series championship to Boston after all these years.' I started typing. John McNamara is a genius.

"The game turns at the end. I'm just about done with the story. I think I used the word 'Einstein' somewhere. Doria comes back. The Red Sox have lost. He says, 'Change your story. Write that John McNamara is an idiot. The moves he's made have lost the Series.'

"Deadline is approaching in five minutes. I don't know what to do. Change my story? I go back and every place I've used the word 'genius' I change it to 'idiot.' I change all the 'dids' to 'didn'ts.' I send in the story. A few days later someone asks McNamara how people have been to him after the Red Sox lost. He says most people have been nice, except for 'a couple of guys in Boston.' I think I know one of them."

These were the Red Sox. They were perpetually in flux. Anything could happen . . . as long as it was bad. A cruel trick always seemed to be played. Geniuses were transformed into idiots in an instant. How many times does a man have to see that same trick not to be fooled again? The con always worked.

The fans somehow stuck with the program. Love often flickered and faltered, but never died. No matter how bad the last heartbreak had been, no matter how many declarations were made that "I will never waste my time with these &*%%$# guys again," spring would arrive and pitchers and catchers would report to work and pictures would begin to come back from Sarasota or Winter Haven or Fort Myers. Hope would begin to grumble like a jelly doughnut in the pits of thousands of stomachs. A new manager, a new shortstop, a young right arm up from Louisville or Pawtucket could make a difference. Couldn't it?

The idea that it all would end, that everyone would get the girl and kiss the horse or whatever happened, was unimaginable. What would it be like? John Glenn or Buzz Aldrin would have to come back and tell us. The losing, the angst, the self-flagellation had become so codified, so structured, that it even had developed marketing names. The suffering was called "The Curse of the Bambino." There was a book about it. There was an HBO movie. The sufferers were called "Red Sox Nation."

Red Sox Nation? What kind of nation was that? Poland? Czechoslovakia? Maybe Northern Ireland, always ruled by a bigger England?

When the end came, swift as it was, eight games in a row, eight wins, a dramatic climb from one of the worst sinkholes of Red Sox history, down three games to none against the accursed Yankees of A-Rod and Derek Jeter and Mr. George Steinbrenner, that made everything even more unimaginable. Is this happening? Is this real?

"I was watching the final game at Mike's Apizza," Ed

Leavitt says. "They're all running on the field and I say, 'Don't believe it until someone shuts the lights off. Things can happen.' I'd seen it too. I once was at Yankee Stadium, last Red Sox–Yankees game of the year. The guy I'm with is a Yankees fan, and we have a bet on the season series. Dinner and drinks. The series is tied, but the Red Sox are winning the game. Someone hits a fly ball to Mike Greenwell for the final out. He catches the ball. The umpire comes running out. Some little kid had wandered onto the field. The umpire had called timeout. Everybody goes back to their places. The guy gets a hit. . . . I'm buying the dinner and drinks."

The skepticism was only natural. After 86 years of disappointment, what sucker could believe the dream was finally coming true? Only 12 nights earlier, the Red Sox had lost to the Yankees, 19–8, at Fenway. Columnist Jim Donaldson in the *Providence Journal* summed up the feeling:

"BOSTON—Johnny Damon may look like a prophet, but his words have proven false," he wrote. "It is not, as he said, the Red Sox are a bunch of idiots. What they are is a bunch of chokes."

The idiots are the ones who truly believed this would be the year the perennially disappointing Sox—who haven't won a World Series since 1918, or even a pennant since 1986—would finally beat the 26-time, world-champion Yankees, who now are on the verge of playing for a 27th title. Only a bunch of idiots would continue to put their faith in this chronically overpaid and underachieving aggregation of ill-kempt characters, this wild-and-crazy bunch of hirsute fun lovers who gleefully pop open champagne bottles to celebrate finishing second for the seventh straight season.

Sure, they're loose. They're also losers.

Doom was in the on-deck circle. The Red Sox were down three games to none against the Yankees. No team in Major League Baseball history had come back from a three-game deficit to win the pennant. Destruction seemed to have already begun. The idea that the Red Sox could come back from *this* did not compute. What happened? Was it, as David Ortiz suggested, that he saw a woman crying after the 19–8 loss and talked about it with his teammates? Was it Damon's simple statement of confidence that "I seem to remember this team has won four games in a row before?" Was it the return of injured pitcher Curt Schilling, the man who talked from the beginning here about sailing into the challenge rather than carrying it on 25 backs? Was it that human femur bone in India?

The slogan Schilling had brought with him from Arizona when he signed with his new (and generous) employer was "Why not us?" This was a question Red Sox fans had asked for ages, but with a different tone, a complaint to the sky, a wonder at why bad things always seemed to happen at the same address and good things always happened at other addresses. Schilling took the plea-bargaining out of the words. Why not us? The question now seemed to be more like a demand.

Three outs were left in the season. A walk, a stolen base, a single, and floodgates opened. Floodgates? There seemed to be pearls on these gates. Trumpets could be heard in the distance. Ortiz was a combination of Babe Ruth and Carl Yastrzemski. Schilling was having his ankle tendon crocheted back into place every few days and throwing bullets. Johnny Damon, who looked like he had been called up from the local slow-pitch league and couldn't come within a foot of a thrown fastball, suddenly was an action hero. He could do anything. The kryptonite was gone.

Pedro was Pedro again. (Glad to have you back.) Manny was Manny. Mark Bellhorn was Sadaharu Oh. Somewhere Derek Lowe seemed to find the talent that he often misplaces—sort of like car keys or spare change on the dresser drawer—and blind opposing batters. Keith Foulke was automatic. Orlando Cabrera was smooth. Trot Nixon and Jason Varitek were anchors. The manager, once known as Terry FranCOMA, became FranCONA again. The Doogie Howser general manager, Theo Epstein, looked young no more. He looked very smart.

One game led into another.

Game four: Boston 6, New York 4 (12 innings)

Game five: Boston 5, New York 4 (14 innings)

Game six: Boston 4, New York 2

Game seven: Boston 10, New York 3

Beating the Yankees, itself, was a wonder on the scale of finding a rent-controlled apartment or parting the Red Sea. An impacted wisdom tooth, a bugger forever, finally had been pulled and the pain was gone. An entire city, an entire region, okay, an entire Red Sox Nation now walked around feeling that weird open space in its mouth. How about that? Wow. There were calls to make to longtime oppressors in Manhattan. Down was up and up was now down. How do you like it down there?

The rest of the road was ridiculously easy.

Game one: Boston 11, St. Louis 9

Game two: Boston 6, St. Louis 2

Game three: Boston 4, St. Louis 1

Game four: Boston 3, St. Louis 0

The emotion of it all could not be denied. Forget that this was the team with the most expensive payroll in baseball history to win a World Series. Forget that no one on the roster came from Boston or Massachusetts or even New England. Forget that teams are put together now on a cash-and-carry annual basis and today's local heroes can be tomorrow's hated villains.

What did the name on the shirts say? Boston Red Sox. Where were the games played? Fenway Park. Somewhere Ted Williams was smiling. Yaz was a champion. Yaz and Rico and Tony C. Jim Lonborg and Jim Ed Rice and Freddie Lynn. Dewey and Butch and Dominic DiMaggio. Johnny and Bobby and Tex Hughson and Mickey McDermott and Bob Stanley and Jerry Adair and Ted Lepcio and Vern Stephens and Pumpsie and Boomer and Bill "Spaceman" Lee. All of them. The water in Boston was poisoned no more. It had turned to champagne.

The news was so different, so strange, that people didn't know what to do, didn't know how to act. Oh, they went through their little celebratory rituals and remembered forgotten friends and family, forgotten times, but what about tomorrow? What about the day after that? World champions. What next?

Lives were given a curious nudge. It didn't feel bad.

"The way I'd learned to deal with everything was to be dispassionate," Ken London, a Boston video producer, says. "I'd watch the big games and tell myself this was no different from a game between San Diego and Milwaukee in June. I was that way in '75 and I was in the bleachers. I was that way in '78. I was working as a social worker at MCI-Walpole. All the residents were going crazy. I held it in. In 1986 I calmly walked up to the television and turned it off.

"That was the way I approached this final game too. Then the Red Sox won and it was 1967 and I was in my garage in Milton, ten years old, looking at my Red Sox yearbook with Yaz and Tony C. on the cover. I could see all the pages in the yearbook. I could see the garage. I hadn't thought about that garage in thirty years. It goes to show you that when you try to control your emotions, you never know where you're going to go when they come out. Hopefully everybody had a happy landing."

What was he wearing in that garage while he looked at his 1967 yearbook?

"A green-and-white striped shirt," he says in an instant. "Green shorts."

The *Boston Globe* ran a headline in huge Kennedy Death type in the morning that said "YES!!!" A fat, wall-to-wall color picture of Jason Varitek and Doug Mientkiewicz and a bunch of other players mobbing reliever Keith Foulke was the major illustration. The smaller headline was "Red Sox complete sweep, win first Series in 86 years." The catchy daily one-word description of the weather at the top of the page, always something to note, was "Sunsational." Columnist Dan Shaughnessy, the author of *The Curse of the Bambino*, the man who gave a name to the collective angst, fittingly enough wrote the lead story.

"ST. LOUIS—They did it for the old folks in Presque Isle, Maine and White River Junction, Vt.," Shaughnessy wrote.

They did it for the baby boomers in North Conway, N.H. and Groton, Mass. They did it for the kids in Central Falls, R.I. and Putnam, Conn.

While church bells rang in small New England towns and horns honked on the crowded streets of the Hub, the 2004 Red Sox last night won the 100th World Series, completing a four-game sweep of the St. Louis Cardinals with a 3–0 victory on the strength of seven innings of three-hit pitching by Derek Lowe. Playing 1,042 miles from Fenway Park, the Sox won it all for the first time in 86 long and frustrating seasons.

The words did the job of expressing local joy quite well, but in these Internet times a parody front page soon was circling in emails. "HOLY SHIT" the headline read in the same Kennedy Death type under the fake *Globe* logo. The caption under the same celebratory photograph read: "The 2004 Red Sox go absolutelyfuckingnuts after winning the World Series in St. Louis." The smaller headline was "Baseball fans the world over express their disbelief. Holy Living Fuck!" The clever weather word was "unfuckingbelievable." The fake Shaughnessy used fewer words in his lead than the real Shaughnessy.

"ST. LOUIS—Jesus fucking Christ," he wrote. "They fucking did it."

The parody probably had the better finger on the pulse of the population.

The following is not a chronicle of the events in October of 2004. An avalanche of books—and time—will take care of that quite nicely. This is a book of the moment. I have interviewed friends, friends of friends, familiar and unfamiliar names around the Red Sox environment, all kinds of people around the scene. No scientific process has been involved. This is a book about how it felt to be a Red Sox fan not only at twenty minutes until midnight on October 27, 2004, but long before that. This is a book about what it all meant.

The stories are the story. I will start with mine.

2. My Story

I STAND WITH MY SON AND MY DAUGHTER AND MY FA-
ther on Boylston Street in Boston on the morning of October 30, 2004. My son is 32 years old, my daughter 29. My father has been dead longer than either of them has been
alive. Let me do the math. What is 1967 from 2004? He has
been dead for 37 years this past February.

"Are you cold?" I ask my daughter, who had a small fever
when she left her house.

She shakes her head. No. Her husband, Doug, was full-
blown sick and couldn't come. No illness short of hospital-
ization was going to keep my daughter home. She says she
dressed in layers. Four layers should be enough.

She has topped off her layers with her "Red Sox Spring
Training" khaki baseball cap that I brought back to her
from Fort Myers, Florida, a number of years ago. Embroidered palm trees are on either side of the olde English red
"B" logo. I'd forgotten I'd even bought it for her. My son
fidgets in the cold with a blue-and-white NFL golf umbrella I brought back from somewhere sometime from
some long-ago event. How'd he ever keep that thing for so
long? A nasty little mist blows almost sideways against our
faces. The umbrella doesn't work.

The crowd awaiting the parade for the world champions—the world champion Boston Red Sox, thank you very much—is maybe ten deep at our spot in front of the Engine 33, Ladder 15 firehouse. We are in the tenth and final row. Some of the firemen have brought out stepladders for their wives and children to get a better view. Vantage points are important. We can see people on the many floors of the open-sided parking garage across the street. People are at the windows in the offices above the Hynes Convention Center. People are on roofs. People are everywhere, as many as 3.5 million people packed along the parade route. Never in history have this many people been in this city at one time.

"Pinky Higgins ought to have his head examined," my father says.

What?

"Pinky Higgins ought to have his head examined," he says again.

A picture flashes. Summer. Cape Cod. The Quaint Steps Cabins. A red plastic radio is on a picnic bench. The melodious voice of sportscaster Curt Gowdy describes some new, but always familiar catastrophe during the 1950s that has happened at Fenway Park. My father is hunched over the picnic bench, unable to sit because the creeping onset of the emphysema that eventually will kill him makes breathing hard in a sitting position. He coughs a lot, blows his nose. He is wearing a sleeveless T-shirt, what they now call a wifebeater, and long dress pants and loafers. Never shorts, even on vacation. His lament about the dumbfounded manager of New England's long-suffering base-

ball team, Michael Franklin Higgins, a redneck from Red
Oak, Texas, a drinking buddy of owner Tom Yawkey, is a
vacation constant.

"Pinky Higgins ought to have his head examined!" I almost shout.

The people on the roofs are pointing now down the
street. Something is coming for sure. The parade was supposed to begin at Fenway, the players and team personnel
loaded onto amphibious vehicles called "ducks," normally
used for a tourist enterprise called Boston Duck Tours. The
ducks will come down Boylston, cut across Tremont Street,
go past City Hall, down Cambridge Street, and into the
Charles River. More people are waiting on the banks of the
river.

"Can you see?" my daughter asks.

"I'm fine," I say.

This is not the truth. I am better than fine.

A love of a sports team is often an inherited passion.
There are other ways to pick a team to follow—ranging
from the bright smile of a certain shortstop to the performance of a football offense against a betting line established
in Las Vegas—but I would guess that the most common
way is to have the team handed down as a family heirloom.
My parents handed me the Catholic Church, the Democ-
ratic Party, and the Red Sox. None of these has been an
easy gift to carry.

My parents were from Northampton, Massachusetts,

which made rooting for the Red Sox natural. They moved to New Haven, Connecticut, where I was born, a place where rooting for the Red Sox was not natural. There is a dividing line somewhere in the middle of Connecticut, probably cutting through the capital, Hartford, where loyalties shift from All Things Boston to All Things New York. New Haven is well south of that line.

The city was predominantly Italian when I grew up, Italian and African American. The Red Sox were not popular with either group. With a long line of Italian stars through the years—Joe DiMaggio and Yogi Berra and Phil Rizzuto, Tony Lazzeri, Frankie Crossetti, even Joe Pepitone—the New York Yankees were logical favorites with one-half of the population. The Brooklyn Dodgers, the team that integrated baseball with Jackie Robinson, then added Roy Campanella and Joe Black and Don Newcombe and Junior Gilliam and other black stars to the roster, were the logical favorites for the other half. The Red Sox, the last team to integrate, slow even in promoting Italian stars, not only were socially backward, they also were terrible. The Yankees won and the Dodgers won (both before and after they left Brooklyn for Los Angeles), and the Red Sox lost. They lost hard. They lost easy. They always lost in the end.

I would find myself, 10 years old, 11 and 12 and beyond, involved in windy arguments that I was doomed to lose. Ted Williams is better than Joe DiMaggio! Ted Williams is better than Mickey Mantle! Ted Williams is better than Mickey Mantle, Duke Snider, and Willie Mays combined! Arguing for the Red Sox was like arguing that the earth was flat. Someone always would come along to point out the curve on the horizon. Someone always would ask which team was now the champion.

I helped a guy named Harry Sitney, who owned a little market called The Grocery Basket on Howe Street. This was fourth or fifth grade. I waited on customers, swept the floor, delivered orders, mostly kept Harry company, and he slipped me five bucks every now and then. He was a Yankees fan, a sportsman, betting on games, always going to the racetrack, a guy who seemed to know how everything worked. I would announce how Al Zarilla was going to bring a pennant, how Don Buddin was the next great shortstop, how Dick Stuart would break Babe Ruth's record. Harry Sitney would laugh. He would challenge me. It was like he had his hand on my head, an adult at arm's length, and I would keep swinging and never hit him.

"What happened to your Red Sox?" was Harry Sitney's perpetual question.

I never had the right answer, the comeback.

"Maybe if we get another pitcher next year . . ."

There always was a maybe.

An only child, I spent a lot of time with the Red Sox in my bedroom. If I see a Topps baseball card from that time, even now, it brings back a surge of memory I can't explain. Someone in the neighborhood had invented a dice baseball game that involved these bubblegum cards. (A 12, boxcars, I remember, was a home run. Snake eyes was a strikeout.) Everyone had teams, leagues, stats to keep in a notebook. Standings. I played game after game, the Red Sox matched against the Yankees or the other teams in the league. The weakness of the game was that all players, good and bad, had the same probabilities. Ted Williams essentially was the same as bonus baby rookie Billy Consolo. The strength of the league was that I controlled all action. Mistakes sometimes happened. No, Ted didn't ground to short. I will roll again for him. He would lead the league in hitting every year.

Every spring for five or six years, I started a scrapbook. I vowed that this was the year for a championship, and I would have a record of all Red Sox games that could be saved forever. I carefully cut out box scores and pasted them into the book. I cut out stories. I kept going until May or June, when the sad course of the present season seemed determined. I never finished a scrapbook, never even reached July.

The games on the radio were magic. It has become a cliché, the romance of listening to baseball on the radio in those early television times, the faraway voice sketching a picture in the imagination, but the romance cannot be denied. I would pretend on those school nights that I was going to bed—good night, see you in the morning—and listen to the voice of Gowdy or Bob Murphy straight from Fenway Park, filtered through the blanket I put over the radio so the light would not shine from under my door. Mythical figures would run across perfect green grass in black polished cleats made of kangaroo leather. Jackie Jensen with his curly blond hair and Sammy White with his sleepy eyes and Jimmy Piersall, the pride of Waterbury, and Ted and steady Frank Malzone and Gene Stephens and Gary Geiger and Jim Gosger and all the rest. Magic.

I saw the Red Sox in person only a handful of times, all

at Yankee Stadium, which was much closer to New Haven than Boston. As the visitors, they always were dressed in utilitarian gray, matched against the white and the pin-stripes of their masters. They were still my boys. I went to Fenway exactly once. It was one of those motor trip vacations into New England, some lake in New Hampshire, I suppose. I only remember the visit to Fenway and the rain. The game was postponed, and my parents agreed to stay another day. The rain did not stop.

I remember we went to Fenway anyway. Just in case. I made my father stand with me outside the gate where the players exited when the game was postponed again, the same gate the players use today. A number of them left in a hurry, into their cars and gone. One stopped. He touched my pen, held it in his hand. He scribbled across my piece of paper. I swear this really happened.

I got Norm Zauchin's autograph.

The little kid who loved the Red Sox later had to go into hiding for a very long time. It was a strange situation. That kid determined what I would do in life—I delivered papers as the little kid and would read the sports page at the end of my route, stare at the head shot of columnist Frank Birmingham in the *New Haven Journal-Courier* as he reported from the Rose Bowl or Belmont Race Track or Fenway itself, and think that he had the greatest job in the world—but I had to leave my old self to do it.

I eventually became a sportswriter at the *Journal-Courier*

and then the *Boston Globe* and then *Sports Illustrated* and learned quickly that sportswriters do not root, do not cheer. (*No Cheering in the Press Box* is the title of a collection of interviews of legendary sportswriters by Jerome Holtzman. It is a statement of the first rule of the business.) To do the job well, a long overcoat of objectivity has to be worn, preferably accompanied by a top hat of cynicism. Would a political reporter root for the candidate he was covering? Would a business reporter root for IBM stock? The accepted logic is that a sports reporter should treat the team he covers no differently.

The little kid would tug at my sleeve every once in a while, wondering what I was doing, but mostly I was able to nudge him away. I first covered a game at Fenway on opening day of 1967, an assignment I caged out of my boss at the *Journal-Courier*. ("Holey-moley, we're in the Red Sox clubhouse," the little kid shouted. "Shut up," I replied.) I was working in Boston by January of 1968.

For the next 21 years I was around the Red Sox a lot. I never was the beat writer for the *Globe*, doing that 162-game annual death march, but I was a columnist, and a columnist in Boston had better spend a lot of time with the Red Sox. I went to spring training most years. I went on a bunch of road trips. I went to most of the big moments. I added about a billion words to the evolving chronicle of frustration.

Let's see. In 1975 I sat with Bernie Carbo as he described his home run in game six with bug-eyed wonder, the one that set the stage for Carlton Fisk's famous shot to win it. Then I winced when Bill Lee threw the eephus pitch to

Tony Perez in game seven. I sat with Carl Yastrzemski after the Bucky Dent playoff game in 1978. Yaz had made the final out, a pop-up. He smoked one Winston after another, drank a Budweiser beer, as he chronicled his emotions. In 1986 . . . ah, I had two-thirds of a celebratory column already written, typing in the basement of Shea Stadium, when a picture on a small black-and-white television with a bad vertical hold seemed to show a baseball going between somebody's legs. I wound up interviewing Bill Buckner.

The players were associates in this little business we shared that involved words. Some of them were nice fellows. Some were not. The games were productions to be analyzed and described. Passion was not part of the operation. I had friends outside the business, Red Sox fans who raged about the important moments, the worst ones, friends who had tales of anguish, who punched walls and drank way too many legal beverages to mute their distress. I did none of that. I was working.

In 1989 I moved along to *Sports Illustrated.* I was removed from Fenway pretty much, talking to marathon runners in South Africa, freestyle wrestlers in Russia, offensive tackles in Cleveland. The magazine had baseball writers who did the baseball stories, and I was a feature writer mostly on faraway assignment. I still watched the Red Sox games on television when I was home, but I no longer was typing out evaluations.

Gradually, a change took place. As each year passed, the distance grew. Turnover in sports is ruthless. The people I knew—the players, the managers, even the front-office personnel—retired or were traded or flat-out fired. The ownership changed. I never had met Nomar Garciaparra. I never had met Pedro Martinez. Roger Clemens, who I knew, was a Toronto Blue Jay and then a Yankee. The little kid began to peek his head out again.

I was in Cleveland, I remember, doing a basketball story on Gordon Gund, the owner of the Cavaliers, when the Red Sox lost the first two games of the 1999 division play-offs to the Cleveland Indians. I was in a bar filled with Indians fans for game two, watching on television. The fans were laughing and yelling, enjoying themselves, and I felt curiously affronted. They were making fun of us. *Us?* Where did that come from? Us? When the Red Sox came back and won the next three games in a row, I felt a charge, a vindication. I bet they're not laughing now!

By the seventh game of the American League Championship Series against the Yankees in 2003, everyone I had known with the Red Sox was gone. The present players were the same as the players I had watched as the little kid, cartoon characters in a communal melodrama. Baseball cards. Names in box scores. I could attribute any qualities I wanted to each of them.

My wife and I watched that ALCS game with my daughter and her husband. He is a disc jockey, doing weddings and bar mitzvahs, corporate events, and part of his equipment is one of those giant projection screens. He had rolled out the screen in his living room so we could watch the game in ten-foot-tall dimensions. He happily promised that he was going to keep it up for the entire World Series.

I rooted just like everyone else. I sat in a lucky seat just like everyone else. When a ten-foot-tall Aaron Boone hit that leadoff home run in the 11th—oh my—I was as quiet as everyone else. The next day my daughter reported that she and her husband had gone to bed shortly after the game ended. In the middle of the night, maybe three or four, she was awakened by a commotion in the living room. Her husband was dismantling the projection screen, putting it away. He said he couldn't endure the sadness of seeing it in the morning.

How about that? I had a story to tell. Just like everyone else.

"There's Johnny Damon," my daughter shouts as the ducks roll past, one after another. "There's Manny. Pedro. Curt Schilling!"

"Isn't that David Ortiz on the other side?" my son says. "See him?"

The ducks are high enough off the ground that we have a very good view of the players. Everyone has a good view. The first duck in the lineup of maybe seven or eight or even ten has music blasting from the speakers, that song about dirty water, down by the River Charles that has become the 2004 anthem, played at heavy-decibel levels after every Red Sox home win. Manny Ramirez is holding a sign that reads "Jeter Is Playing Golf. This is better," a reference to the Yankees shortstop and the Yankees' not-so-sad fate. Pedro is dancing. Schilling is waving and smiling. The sound of the cheering, mixed with the music, bounces off the city walls and bounces back and bounces back again. Someone has shot off a confetti cannon on one of the ducks, and I have pieces of red, white, and blue paper stuck to my zipper jacket.

It is all wonderful. There is a feeling of . . . I suppose the proper word is "completion." Eighty-six years. How many people have said, "I hope they just win the damn thing during my lifetime?" Okay, the Red Sox have won the damn thing during my lifetime. They have. I saw it. Here is proof.

"I remember the time you took me to spring training," my daughter says. "Down in Winter Haven? We were at the pool at the motel, and Oil Can Boyd was there. I wanted to get his autograph. I asked you if I could. You said, 'Sure, ask him.' I didn't want to. I was so nervous. I finally went over there and he couldn't have been nicer. Signed my paper. Talked with me."

One duck is filled with former Red Sox players. Dennis "Oil Can" Boyd is one of them. He is waving. Who else? There's Rich Gedman. There's Johnny Pesky. There's what's-his-name. There's . . . the duck is gone too fast.

"Remember the '86 World Series?" my son, who now lives in New York, says. "You came down from the press box to sit with us? Everyone was yelling at Darryl Strawberry. 'Darrrrryl. Darrrrryl. . . .'"

I stand with my two children, both of them grown and happy. It is all quite wonderful. They have inherited the love that I inherited. I stand with my father, dead for all these years. (He likes this. He even forgives Pinky Higgins.) I stand with Harry Sitney, long gone. (I have the answer, at last, to what happened to the Red Sox, Harry. They won.) Different people flash in and out. A lifetime of people. I suppose I am like everyone here. The crowd might be listed as 3.5 million, but hasn't everyone brought along someone else who "really would have loved to see this"? Maybe a bunch of someone elses? How large would the crowd be if all the someone elses were counted? Ten million? More than that.

I wear a Red Sox cap. Not the official cap. This one, same regulation blue, has a pair of embroidered red socks, the team logo, on the front. I never owned a Red Sox cap, all those years as a Boston sportswriter, feeling it would be very unprofessional to wear a team hat, and in a way I don't feel that I own this one.

I bought it in the fall of 2002 for Jack Benoit. He was a guy from my boyhood neighborhood in New Haven, a good basketball player, a good hockey player, a good guy. A dice baseball player! There was a bunch of us who hung around together at Bobby and Dickey Montgomery's house at 51 Garden Street. We called ourselves the Garden Street Athletic Club, maybe 20 or 30 neighborhood urchins, playing sports, talking sports, growing up and finally moving out.

The bonds were strong enough that we have stayed in touch, stayed together through marriages and divorces, through kids and assorted jobs and assorted careers, all the way. Jack Benoit worked for the Southern New England Telephone Company as a lineman for a while, then opened his own landscaping business. He raised a couple of sons, coached some teams, mowed all the appropriate grown-up lawns. He became, just three years ago, the first of us to become really sick.

He had a brain tumor, and he had the operation, and after the operation didn't work he had the chemo and the radiation or whatever it is. His body shut down on him in pieces, but his determination and his optimism never stopped. He was in the hospice in Connecticut, and everyone knew what that meant, when he talked about buying a Red Sox cap. It was part of his determination and optimism.

"I'm going to opening day at Fenway," he said in his bed. "I'm going to take the train and get off at Back Bay Station, and Monk is going to meet me, and I'm going to buy a Red Sox cap and we're going to go to opening day."

Nicknames never leave. I was Monk. I heard about what Jack said, and I went to the Twins souvenir stand across from Fenway and bought the hat. I was going to bring it to the hospice—"Here, you've got the hat already, Jackie. Just get yourself out of this place and come to the game"—but never had a chance. He died on November 12, 2002.

I suppose I could have given the hat to his widow, Angela, but there seemed no point. I kept it. I hardly ever wore it—still feeling unprofessional—but on this day I did.

The final duck comes past, the end of the parade, and I find myself waving Jack Benoit's hat in the air. Waving it around and around and around. I never have done something like that. Never.

My son and daughter laugh at me. Very unprofessional.

3. The Boston Baseball Story

Following the Red Sox in Boston always has seemed different from the way people followed other teams in other cities around the country. There never has been that oom-pah feel of boosterism, that rah-rah mentality. The Red Sox have been more like family, like being around that slightly different second cousin from Chelsea, the one who wears his pants a few inches too short, who smiles at the wrong time, who has to be defended because he's a blood relation.

"He's not a bad kid. You just have to get to know him . . . "

"He has his ways. He's not hurting anybody . . . "

Pictures sometimes come onto the television screen from a place like St. Louis, and everyone will be dressed in red and a sign on the message board will say CLAP and everybody will clap. Following the Red Sox never has been like that.

The Red Sox fan never has been part of an organized religion, everyone showing up for church on a double-header Sunday. He has been defensive much more than offensive, understated much more than overstated. He has had his quiet conversations with a personal God—or Ted Williams or Carlton Fisk or Manny Ramirez. (Please get a hit, Manny. Please. Please.) He mostly has crossed his fingers, crossed his toes, and wondered out loud why the blunder-boy manager has removed (or not removed) the pitcher.

Maybe it has been the losing, the history, that created this intimate feeling. Maybe it has been the area, New England skepticism on parade again. No chamber of commerce yahoos allowed. Maybe it has been the fact that Fenway Park doesn't have a second deck, that from the street it looks like a warehouse instead of some grand citadel of sport.

Whatever the case, the Red Sox never have been some special show. They simply have been . . . here. If you grew up in Boston or Malden, Medford or East Bridgewater, Newton or Newburyport, you were handed winters that froze your nose off, summers on Cape Cod, backups on the Southeast Expressway, an intriguing cast of characters on Beacon Hill, and the Red Sox.

They always have been a big deal, perhaps . . . but without ever being a big deal. A Boston thing.

❖

Don Gavin (comedian):

"There was a guy in West Roxbury named George Burns, but everybody called him 'Crazy G,'" Don Gavin says. "That was his license plate, CRAZYG. He drove a big green Cadillac, a convertible. If you wanted to go to the

Red Sox game as a kid, you waited in front of Charlie's on Center Street and Crazy G showed up around one o'clock for a one-thirty game.

"The trip from West Roxbury to Fenway Park should take about forty-five minutes, but he'd do it in eighteen. He never had to buy a full set of tires because he only used two at a time. He'd just come flying around the Jamaicaway, eighty-five miles an hour. Never had an accident that I know of.

"You had to pay Crazy G fifty cents to go to the game. That included the ride. He had ushers all over the place. I don't know what he paid them, but we paid him fifty cents. He'd have eight, nine kids in the Cadillac, and we'd all get in."

This was Boston baseball for a long time. Every neighborhood in the sixties had a Crazy G, someone who knew the back doors and the proper palms to find. Fenway Park was a land of winks and nods. You'd buy your peanuts on the street. Cheaper. Buy your sausage on the street. Better. Go see Mr. So-and-So. He'll get you in.

The flannel shirts from Maine and New Hampshire and Agawam would arrive on buses, filled with wonder and Elks Club beer. Fenway was a melting pot. Characters from Charles Dickens did business with characters from Mickey Spillane. Characters from Henry James or John Cheever might show up from time to time, good seats, the big games at the big moments, but the lifeblood of the operation ran through the shadows.

"A ticket to the bleachers, a real ticket, was two dollars," Don Gavin says. "So you could go to the game legitimately if you had the two dollars. Going with Crazy G, though, you'd get into some of the real good seats. A lot of those rich people in those days never went to the games. I sat in one seat so often that when the real people came one day, the usher wouldn't believe they owned the tickets. He said, 'This kid's here every day.'"

Gavin, 55 years old, grew up in this land of winks and nods. They are a foundation for his street-smart act. He started out with Jackie Jensen as an idol—"Jackie Jensen was good at both football and baseball, and I wasn't good at either of them, so I figured he should be my idol"—and went from there. He has been a lifetime follower of the Red Sox and has acquired the requisite memories.

In 1967, the last day of the season, when Jim Lonborg was carried through the air, Gavin was on the field with every other kid at the park. In 1975 and Carlton Fisk, he was in real seats. In 1986 he was in New York for the last two games of the World Series. Working.

"A guy in New York figured it would be a good idea to have three Boston comedians appearing while the games were played," Gavin says. "It was a place called Stand-Up New York. Dennis Leary opened, then Tony V, then me as the headliner—that'll show you how times change. First night, game six is going on. Each of us, when we go out, delivers a report on the game, about how it's going. The way it worked out, each of us reported the Red Sox were winning. This was a report to all these New York people who loved the Mets, hated the Red Sox. The show ended, and the game was still going on. The Red Sox were still winning.

"I bought three bottles of Moet champagne. I don't

know how much it cost, but it was more than I was making for the night. We go out there, all these New York people, and a waiter has the caps off and is going to open the champagne. It's the ninth inning and the Mets are at bat, and I say, 'No, no, hold off.' One out. 'No, no.' Two outs. 'Not yet.'

"What happens next happens, and the New York people are cheering and the waiter says, 'What do you want me to do with these bottles of champagne?' Tony V says, 'Stick 'em up your ass.'"

Gavin was around Fenway for the stretch run of 2004, working in the movie *Fever Pitch* with Drew Barrymore and Jimmie Fallon. He played a Boston cop who runs across the field, chasing Barrymore. The movie's plot relied on the Sox's losing tradition, so when they won, the directors had to rewrite the ending in a hurry. Gavin had to return to reshoot the ending.

In the waiting time before his scene he got to walk across the "sacrosanct turf," throw off the mound, look inside the scoreboard in the Green Monster. It was a kick. The Red Sox have been a fun part of life.

"I've never been part of the anger that's developed," he says. "I never understood it. You'd go to a game against the Baltimore Orioles, and all these kids would start yelling, 'Yankees suck.' Well, first of all, the Yankees don't suck. They've won the World Championship twenty-six times. Second, they aren't here. The Baltimore Orioles are here. All this anger . . . what was it about? If anything, you'd think people would have become acclimated to the losing, not angry."

For the final moment, the World Series win, he was on a cruise ship. He works cruise ships 30 weeks a year now telling his Boston stories. He went to his state room to watch game three and then game four from St. Louis. Reception sometimes fades on the ships, and both nights it faded after the first three or four innings. He sat in the room with the static running across the screen during game four, waiting for the reception to return. He thought about Crazy G.

"He'd pull up at Fenway and park anywhere he wanted, and he never would get a ticket," Gavin says. "He'd park at fire hydrants, handicapped spots for crippled people. I think once he parked on top of a crippled person. He was a character. A gambler. Went to the Red Sox every day. Ask anyone in West Roxbury about him. I majored in psychology in college. I talked to him once for a paper I was doing, asked him, 'What's your idea of a perfect day?' He said, 'There's a hurricane and I'm walking down Center Street smoking a big cigar, watching people get pissed off.' He didn't hesitate with his answer. It's like he had it planned. Crazy G."

The static on the television in the state room on the ship never left. The game never returned. After a couple of hours Gavin figured the game must be finished and made a phone call to catch the result. The ship-to-shore rate is $8.95 per minute. He had to get the details. Learning that the Red Sox had won the World Series cost him $184.

"Plus, I had bet St. Louis all four games," he says. "I didn't want to jinx the Red Sox. So I'm out $184 plus the bets and the Red Sox finally have won the World Series. Figures."

Dick Johnson (curator, New England Sports Museum):

"Nobody ever mentions baseball before 1900," Dick Johnson says. "It's like it didn't exist. Well, it did exist. There was a lot of baseball before 1900, and Boston was the center of it all. The Cincinnati Red Stockings, the first professional team in the United States, disbanded and all the players came to Boston. Starting in 1876, the team from Boston in the National League won twelve pennants in twenty-five years. In a forty-nine-year period, up until 1918, teams from Boston won twenty-one titles in five different major leagues.

"What I'm saying is that we come from rich baseball blood around here. Those percentages are better than any comparable period for any team, even the Yankees. This is a city that always has loved it, loved baseball."

Johnson, 48, fell in love with the game during the summer of Tony Conigliaro and Yaz, 1967. He remembers throwing a tennis ball against the family garage in Worcester, listening to Ernie Harwell in Detroit describe the final game of the season between the Tigers and the Angels. The Red Sox already had won, beating the Twins, and now everything rested on this game in faraway Detroit. Tigers win, there is a playoff. Tigers lose, the Red Sox are American League champions, off to meet the Cardinals in the World Series.

Who could resist the suspense? When Dick McAuliffe of the Tigers—who never grounded into a double play—grounded into a double play to finish the game, Angels win, happiness reigned in Worcester. This was when, Johnson says, the Red Sox went from black-and-white to color, sort of like *The Wizard of Oz*. The 1967 finish began the transformation into what they are today, changed everything "competitively, financially, spiritually."

"The charm of the Red Sox against the Yankees is that for the Red Sox to win, they always have to be smarter," he says. "Smarter and prescient enough to cut through all the cronies, all the nonsense. They're never going to have the money the Yankees have, but they can win the battle by firing less bullets and capturing more troops. I've always loved the cartoons by Bill Gallo in New York showing George Steinbrenner in a spiked helmet. That's perfect. They have the spiked helmet. We have a green eyeshade. That's how we have to win."

As the longtime spirit of the New England Sports Museum, guiding the operation through various venues until it finally reached its present home at the Fleet Center, Johnson wound up answering historical questions during the 2004 run through the playoffs. He also found himself sending newspapers around the country to friends and acquaintances who said, "Send me the *Globe*, send me the *Herald*." In three weeks of postseason baseball, he estimates he spent over $200 in postage. Just for newspapers.

"My brother was visiting from the West Coast when the Red Sox won it," Johnson says. "That was great. It just happened that way. He's eight years older than I am, so he's been following it all longer than I have. He goes from Chuck Schilling to Curt Schilling. It was a perfect situation. We sat around, told the stories."

The best one was from 1986. (Aren't the best stories always from 1986 for Red Sox fans?) Johnson was one of the more resilient people in Boston after the Buckner Moment in game six. He figured that there still was another chance in game seven. He approached it with the same optimism he had for game six.

The appearance of Al Nipper on the mound in the third or fourth inning brought all that optimism to a halt. Nothing personal, but Johnson was not a fan of Al Nipper. He didn't know what to do with his worry and disgust—Al Nipper is pitching the seventh game of the World Series!—but he knew he couldn't watch television any longer. He grabbed his radio and headphones and went to the door.

"Where are you going?" his wife Mary asked.

"I don't know," Johnson replied. "Out. Somewhere. I'm just walking."

He lived on Beacon Hill and headed west, the game now played through the headphones as he wandered through a dreary mist. One step after another took him to Beacon Street, and then he crossed over to Commonwealth Avenue and suddenly he had a direction. He realized he was headed toward Fenway Park.

If the Red Sox won, well, he would be there for what surely would be a celebration. If the Red Sox didn't win, well, at least he wouldn't be home for the phone calls from friends in New York. He was sitting on the steps of the Red Sox offices at 4 Yawkey Way for the final inning and a half of the 8–5 loss that finished the Series.

"I was all alone," he says. "That sort of surprised me.

Now, of course, there'd be all kinds of stuff, the sky-eye helicopters and the television reporters doing their live reports on location, but there was none of that. I was sitting on the steps between the two copper gates of the Red Sox offices, smiling bas-reliefs on Eddie Collins and Tom Yawkey on either side of me."

A 20th anniversary party for the *Boston Phoenix* was being held with an A-list group of Boston makers and shakers in attendance at a nightclub around the corner on Lansdowne Street, so the parking places on the street all were filled. One nice car was parked behind another. A young guy suddenly appeared—another fan, perhaps—and walked down the street. He stopped at a high-priced Volvo. He kicked open the side window. He reached inside and pulled out the stereo. He started running.

Johnson sat where he was, alone again. The postgame show with local talk-show host Eddie Andelman was now in his ears. ("Would you have brought in Nipper?" "No, I wouldn't, Eddie.") The Volvo's security alarm was beeping. The Red Sox were dead, and Johnson had to walk home through the rain.

He says he felt like he had been dropped into an Edward Hopper painting.

Ian Thomsen (father of Christopher Thomsen, elementary school student):

"We were at my in-laws in Winthrop this summer, and I made a mistake," Ian Thomsen says. "I got there late, and I told Chris I'd heard on the radio the Red Sox had traded Nomar. I should have waited until we got home. He just started crying. It was awful. He cried and cried. We went home and he still cried. He cried for a week.

"He'd just be sitting on the couch by himself and tears would be rolling down his face. I'd go over to him and say, 'What is it? Is it Nomar?' He'd shake his head and keep crying."

The deal that perhaps seemed easy for Red Sox general manager Theo Epstein at the July 31 trading deadline—Nomar still seems injured, Nomar is unhappy, Nomar will be a free agent at the end of the season—was not so easy for Red Sox fan Chris Thomsen, age eight, to swallow. He is a throwback kind of a kid, more interested in the people and events at Fenway than in the latest PlayStation game or the soap-opera stories of big-time wrestling. Baseball is his unconditional love.

Under the rules of unconditional love, when a star leaves after he has been with your team for as long as you have been alive, when you have perfected imitations of all of his idiosyncrasies—gloves on, gloves off, everything just right—when you have stood at Fenway and shouted his name and are sure that he heard you, it is a major shock. Tears are necessary. Maybe Nomar is crying too? Tears should join with tears. Maybe a letter would do the job.

"Chris sat at the dining room table with Maureen, my wife," Ian Thomsen says. "He wrote the whole thing by himself. He was sniffling and tearing up and blowing his nose the whole time. (A box of tissues was on the table nearby.) He was kneeling on one of those big dining room chairs with his arms on the table, leaning directly over the paper, so that you could make out the faint outline of his teardrops on the original handwritten letter that he put in the mail to Nomar, courtesy of the Chicago Cubs, Wrigley Field, etc., etc."

This was the letter:

Dear Nomar:

Thanks for everything you've done here in Boston. I think you're the best shortstop the Red Sox ever had. I went to the game where you hit your last grand slam on the Red Sox with my friend Michael, my dad and my friend's dad. I was so excited! You have always been my favorite player and I have called myself "NOMAR" since kindergarten. (I'm going into third grade.) I will always love you even if you're a Chicago Cub.

If you want write back please write to:

Christopher Thomsen

[address]

Maybe I will go to Chicago to a Cubs game. I'll be the one wearing the Red Sox Garciaparra shirt. I hope you come back to Boston. Have fun with Todd Walker. (My mom loves him.)

Sincerely,

Christopher Thomsen ☺

The odd part to all this was that when rumors first had begun about a possible trade in the off-season to obtain Alex Rodriguez, Christopher had not minded. The deal seemed balanced, a superstar for a superstar. That was acceptable. Nomar would not feel disrespected in that kind of deal.

"Baseball is all about the people to Chris, not the institution," Ian Thomsen says. "Like I was worried in 2003, when Aaron Boone hit the home run. I thought Chris would be crying when I told him. It didn't bother him at all.

"This year we went to game three of the Yankees series, the 19–8 blowout. Didn't faze him. He was happy just going to his first Yankees game. People left early, so we moved around to different seats in the ballpark. We stayed until the end, and Chris was happy all the way."

Chris Thomsen went to bed at his normal time on the night of the final game of the World Series. His father watched a lot of the game from the porch. He had a good view of the lunar eclipse, so he watched the moon and the game, back and forth, always looking through the window to see Trot Nixon hit another double off the wall on the television screen. When the ninth inning came, he and his wife awakened Chris and their ten-year-old daughter Jacqueline.

Maureen had started a family celebration tradition when the Patriots won their first Super Bowl, picking each kid up and throwing them on the couch. When the final out was made, cheering everywhere, she picked up Jacqueline, picked up Chris, threw them on the couch. Everybody then went to a neighbor's house where the kids drank diet Sprite from champagne glasses.

An addendum: A day or two later, somewhere around the house Ian Thomsen found one of those little blowout cards that are stuffed in magazines. This one was for *Sports*

Illustrated for Kids. Chris Thomsen already receives *SI for Kids*, but nevertheless he had filled out the card. On one half, under the instructions "Send To:" were his neatly printed name and address. On the other half, under the instructions "Bill To:" were the neatly printed words "Derek Jeter, Bronx, N.Y."

❖

Joe O'Donnell (chairman, Boston Culinary Group):

"Here's the first thought I had when the fourth game of the World Series ended: now I'm no longer interested in owning the Red Sox," Joe O'Donnell says. "I had kept the idea in my subconscious that it still could happen, but the reason for wanting to own the team was to be the guy who brought the championship to Boston. My appetite for stepping into the arena now was gone."

A second thought also slipped into his head: I have just made a lot of money.

"I was in Las Vegas before the playoffs started," O'Donnell says. "I really thought this was the team that was going to do it. This was the year. I made some substantial investments to back that thought and got some very good odds. It was three and a half to one for winning the pennant, six and a half to one for the World Series. There was a lot of money involved."

A 60-year-old self-made millionaire in the concessions business who started his entrepreneurial career by renting out tuxedos for his senior prom at Malden Catholic High School, O'Donnell was the local suitor when the Red Sox were up for sale in 2001. He and partner Steve Karp were the ones who had chewed on the local disappointments for a lifetime. They were the ones who knew—really knew—what a big deal winning it all in Boston would be like.

"I used to go to the games all the time as a kid. My Little League coach was an usher, and he'd sneak us in the back into the bleachers. I grew up in Everett. We'd take the T. This was when we were ten years old, eleven. We'd go in all by ourselves. The big thing was getting from the bleachers into the good seats. There was a fence with a guard. We called it 'The Continental Divide.' We'd hang around and hang around until there was a rush of people, and we'd slip through in a crowd. Or we'd wait until the usher took a break and leave the gate open. We'd go by most of the time . . . and if we didn't, we'd sit in the front row of the bleachers. I loved to watch Mickey Mantle out there when he came to town."

The long-ago innocence strikes him. What kids do that now, go to a baseball game three and four and five times a week at ten and eleven years old? What kids ten and eleven years old go anywhere alone anymore? The prices are too high, the games too late, most of them at night, for kids to be regulars. The world is too threatening for kids to explore.

"My friend Carl Canderosi and I would go from Everett to the Charlestown Boys Club to go swimming," he says. "All it cost was ten cents, a nickel for the T each way. The first time we went we got the shit beat out of us. These Charlestown kids, older, see us coming down the steps of the Boys Club. We were wearing our Everett Little League caps. One of the kids says to Carl, 'What's the E stand for, Eat It?' I'll never forget that. They ripped the bill right off my hat. I went home wearing the hat without a bill. It looked like a yarmulke.

"Later on, we got to know those kids. We became friends. That was the way it was."

The long-ago memories and entrepreneurial instincts brought him into the bidding for the Red Sox. He had plans that included a new ballpark on the Fan Pier in South Boston. He thought he had a shot. The deal made sense because his company is one of the largest ballpark concessionaires in the country.

On the night before the bids were due to be submitted, the lame-duck Red Sox administration signed a ten-year concessions deal with one of O'Donnell's competitors. O'-Donnell could see that the old Continental Divide had been resurrected at Fenway, and this time nobody was going to leave the gate unguarded. He and Karp were on the outside.

"It was such a screw job," he says. "Everybody in town knew it was a screw job. [Commissioner of baseball] Bud Selig wanted these guys from small-market cities to get the team. He didn't care about local ownership."

O'Donnell has watched the small-market guys—John Henry, Tom Werner, and Larry Lucchino—with interest. He likes a lot of what they have done. He likes John Henry, sits with him in the owner's box sometimes, neither of them saying much, just watching baseball and enjoying what they see. He marvels at their good fortune.

What would have happened in 2003 if the Oakland A's

had completed a sweep, three and out, hadn't suffered assorted brain locks in that third game? There would have
been no Yankees series, no seven games. Fenway never
would have been sold out for the next season. What would
have happened if the Yankees had completed the sweep in
2004, if Mariano Rivera had gone one-two-three in the
ninth inning of the fourth game? The talk would have been
all about the 19–8 drubbing, the sweep, the ignominious
finish. The sports business operates on strange, thin mar-
gins.

What would have happened if the Boston guy had been
able to buy the team?

"I've thought about that," Joe O'Donnell says. "I don't
know if we would have won it all or not, but I do know we
would have been going into a new stadium. Fenway Park
would be done."

4. The Old Story

THE RED SOX ALWAYS WERE INTERESTING. THAT WAS their enduring quality. Sometimes they were bad, sometimes good, sometimes very good . . . just never quite good enough. But they always entertained. Even when they were bad, terrible, they always had at least a couple of marquee players, all-stars, hitters, people to see. The short left-field wall at Fenway made hitters, and hitters made headlines.

Ted Williams was a hitting virtuoso through the forties and fifties, a show by himself, controversial and opinionated, in trouble and out, handsome as the dickens, the best drawing card in baseball. In the sixties and into the seventies, there was Yaz. Every kid in New England had the batting stance, hands held high, just like Yaz. Who didn't want to be Yaz? Carlton Fisk and Jim Ed Rice followed, and there was Freddie Lynn and Dwight Evans and Wade Boggs and one Red Sox team after another that had a leading man, a leading light. Nomar Garciaparra was a star from the moment he stepped onto the field at Fenway.

There always were people to talk about. There always were situations. There always was something.

Joe Camacho (retired):

"Watching those games this year, all I could think about was how much Ted would have liked all this," Joe Camacho says. "That's my biggest regret, that he wasn't around to see it. I'm sure he would have had some of those [foul] words of his to describe everything. As it is, I'll bet he probably went from upside down to right side up in that thing in Arizona."

Joe Camacho, 76, probably was Ted Williams's best friend. In the last years of Williams's life, Camacho would get on the phone in Fairhaven, Massachusetts, and Williams would get on the phone in Hernando, Florida, and they would watch Red Sox games together long-distance. Williams would offer loud and salty opinions about everything that happened. Camacho would counter quietly. Williams, even after his three strokes, half-blind, would boom back.

Even during the 2004 World Series, two years after Williams's death, his voice was heard in Camacho's living room. Camacho watched every game with his son Jimmy, who works in state auditor Joe DeNucci's office, and Ted was always with them.

"Ted would have loved to see them beat the Yankees," Camacho says. "Down deep, I don't think he liked the Yankees. He'd always talk about 'that goddamned Casey Stengel, never gave me shit to hit.' He would have been pleased.

"We'd have been talking back and forth about the hitters. I wanted to ask him, in fact, about Johnny Damon.

How can a guy look so horseshit for three games, missing a ball by a foot, then come back and hit the way he did? I couldn't figure it out. Ted would have had an opinion."

Camacho was a ballplayer as a young man, playing in the farm systems of the St. Louis Browns and the Cleveland Indians. An ankle injury ended his career in the minors, and he became a teacher and then a high school principal. He worked summers at the Ted Williams Camp in Lakeville, and that was where he met the Red Sox slugger. They became friends. When Williams took a job with the Washington Senators, managing in the major leagues, he took Camacho with him as a bench coach to handle the positioning of the players, to lay out strategy.

Camacho was a lifelong Red Sox fan, "dying like we all did" at the major moments. Ted was Ted. He always wondered out loud why Camacho didn't make the major leagues. He always answered his own question, said it probably was because Camacho was "too f———n dumb."

"I used to work out with the Indians at Fenway Park," Camacho says. "I was going to Bridgewater State, and they let me finish the term every year before reporting to the minor leagues. When the Indians came to town, I worked out with them. Bobby Avila—did you see he just died?—and Al Smith would give me their new shoes to break in. I'd wear the shoes, then give them back.

"I was hitting one day and I caught a ball on the trademark, and it went over the wall in left. Didn't even hit it hard. That wall was so close. You didn't even have to hit it hard."

The living room formation for watching the heroics in

2004 was Joe on the couch, Jimmy on the recliner, no changes.

Joe decided that Ted's favorite player probably would have been David Ortiz. He would have liked Ortiz's free-swinging approach coupled with enough control to lay off bad pitches. Jimmy wondered if Ted would have been upset with all the long hair and the scruffy appearances of the Red Sox. Ted was military. He never liked long hair. Joe said that the baseball would have won out.

When the final out was made in St. Louis, the bachelor father and the bachelor son stood and shook hands. They both said the same thing.

"I wonder what Ted's thinking right now?"

Joe Morgan (retired):

"I first saw a Red Sox game in 1938, when I was seven years old," Joe Morgan says. "My father worked on weekends and we didn't own an automobile, so we didn't go much. When we did, they always seemed to be playing the Philadelphia Athletics. The Red Sox would schedule the bad teams during the week, often for doubleheaders. I saw a lot of the Philadelphia Athletics in doubleheaders because we always went on Mondays or Tuesdays, my father's days off. That was all right. My father loved Connie Mack because he was Irish.

"A bus ran from Providence to Boston and stopped in Walpole. That's how we would get to the games. It cost $1.06, round trip. We'd get off at Wentworth Institute and walk. The trick was getting the bus back. It stopped first at Park Square, and sometimes it was packed before it got to Wentworth Institute. The bus driver wouldn't even open the door. He'd make a signal with his thumb backwards, like another bus was coming. Yeah, it might be coming, but not for a long, long time."

Morgan, 74, wound up being a career baseball man. He played for four teams in four years in the majors, hitting .193 as a utility infielder, and had a long career in the minors. He then coached and managed in the minors, managing the AAA Pawtucket Red Sox for a number of years. It was an enjoyable life, no regrets, and in the middle of 1988 it took an unexpected turn. He became the manager of the Red Sox. He was 57 years old and had thought that any hope of managing in the big leagues was gone.

"It all started when Rene Lachemann, the third-base coach, took a job that year with the Oakland A's," Morgan says. "They brought me up to coach third. In the middle of the season the team wasn't doing very well, and they fired John McNamara the day after the All-Star Game. They made me the interim manager. I guess whoever was the third-base coach was going to become the interim manager. I was the third-base coach."

Morgan looked at the coming schedule—an 11-game home stand to start the second half of the season—and figured he had to win at least 7 games to have a chance of finishing the season in the manager's office. There already were rumors that management was talking with Joe Torre, who was available. The Red Sox players took care of all decisions. They won all 11 games at home, and another on the road before losing. They won 19 of Morgan's first 20. He was the interim manager no more and wound up in charge for the next four years.

Managing the Red Sox often is called the toughest job in Boston, but Morgan never felt that way. He never worried about what he said. He never worried about what he did. He was too old for all of that stuff. He simply did the best he could.

"Here's the way to manage in Boston: you have to have faith in yourself," he says. "If you do something and it works, okay. If it doesn't work, you just have to have faith in what you're doing. You have to please yourself and not worry about anybody else.

"Here's the story with all decisions you make, like Grady Little deciding to leave Martinez in that game last year: you never know what you're going to do until you do it. I remember a thing Birdie Tebbetts once said—that if your best pitcher is out there and they're getting all these cheap hits off him, bloops and check swings, you probably should take him out because it's just not his day. I think that's probably right, but you never know until you're there what you're going to do."

Morgan never bought the idea that the pressures of playing at Fenway in front of a demanding audience affected the performance of the team. Bruce Hurst, the pitcher, once told him he didn't like pitching at Fenway. Morgan told him, "What's the problem? We score six runs for you in the first inning. You hold the other team to five. We win the game." The road was the bigger problem. All of those traditional Fenway power teams built to knock down the fences had burnouts when they played in places where the fences weren't as close.

"That was the story with a lot of teams," Morgan says. "Never any speed. That was the story of eighty-six years. And 1986, that thing was just a freak happening. They should have won it."

Morgan groused through the 2004 Series about the length of the players' pants, no sock at all showing for players like Ramirez and Martinez ("Wear the uniform!"). He was fascinated by Mark Bellhorn. ("No player in baseball history ever has had the season he had. Led the league in strikeouts, but walked a lot, hit homers, and had a .265 average.") He cringed at all the talk about pitch counts.

"I'd like to see guys pitch longer," he says. "Like Mike Mussina bailed out after six innings. What was that? He should be ashamed. Guys pitch six innings now, and they go in the clubhouse and do somersaults because they know they can't lose. Pitch the game!"

There was a part of Morgan that wanted to see the Cardinals rally in the Series, bring everything back to Fenway for the close. There was a bigger part that liked what he saw.

"Never," the former manager says, "give a sucker a second break."

Clark Booth (writer, broadcaster):
"There never was any Mickey Mouse curse with the Red

Sox," Clark Booth says. "I hate those easy, quick explanations. They cover up sixty to seventy years of monumental incompetence with this franchise. If there was any curse, it was the Curse of Tom Yawkey. There was always a decadence around this team, an awful lot of odd behavior that had nothing to do with any freakin' curse.

"For thirty years, Yawkey had only one way of building a team: sign a $60,000 check (which was a lot of money at the time) for someone like Matt Batts. There was no plan. It wasn't just racism against blacks that hurt the Red Sox. Eddie Collins hated Catholics for a long time. Yawkey hated Jews. These people hated everybody."

For Booth, a longtime television reporter in Boston with WCVB and a columnist for the Catholic newspaper *The Pilot*, the Red Sox were never a star-crossed operation. They were bumblers and stumblers, everything run in secret as if this were some kind of fraternal lodge instead of a business model. Skeletons hung in half the closets. The other half were stocked with liquor.

The team, for the longest time, was run in a fine alcoholic mist. Yawkey was the owner from 1933 until his death in 1976. His wife Jean was an owner from 1976 until her death in 1992. And the Jean Yawkey Trust was the owner until 2002. Tom Yawkey was a drinker. His wife was a drinker. The general managers uniformly were drinkers. The managers often were drinkers. The press room had a bar, open before and long after games, and was filled with drinkers. Walter Underhill, the bartender, poured with a steady and heavy hand. Discussions were noisy.

Booth arrived on the scene in the sixties, fresh from Holy Cross College, amazed at how it worked.

"The guy who finally made some sense out of it all was [general manager] Dick O'Connell," Booth says. "He was a drinker too, but he had a business mind. He took the race issue head on, signed Reggie Smith, Joe Foy, George Scott, brought in Elston Howard. It was as easy as that. No more race issue.

"He was a brilliant guy. He was chief of naval intelligence at Pearl Harbor in World War II. He had a saying . . . some young reporter like Peter Gammons would be asking him a lot of questions and leave and O'Connell would turn to you and say, 'He thinks this fucking shit is real.' He said that all the time: 'He thinks this fucking shit is real.' But he was the one who turned it around.

"The place was filled with some wonderful characters, but underneath it all there was this strain of darkness with the Yawkeys. It was all very weird."

Booth has waited for years for the secrets all to fall out of the closet, tumble into public view, but that never has happened. It probably never will happen now. Virtually all of the characters have died, and now, with the quest for a World Championship finished, a more flattering light of history will shine on everything that happened before. Attention will move to other places.

That was why Booth kicked a footstool in his house in New Smyrna, Florida, when Kevin Millar walked in the ninth inning of game four against the Yankees. He felt, just like that, the long story might end. The easy veil of winning and all the blather about curses would cover what really happened. And now we'll never know.

"How long have the new owners been here?" Booth says. "Three years. That's how long it took once the Yawkey organization was out of the picture. That's your curse that has bothered this team forever."

❖

Bill Lee (perpetual baseball player):

Bill Lee pitched for the Red Sox from 1969 until 1978, then pitched four more years with the Montreal Expos. His career record for 14 seasons was 119–90 with a 3.62 ERA. He started the seventh and deciding game against the Cincinnati Reds in the 1975 World Series, but left with no decision. His nickname is "Spaceman."

"I watched the seventh game of the Yankees series in a bar in downtown Maui," Bill Lee says. "My oldest daughter was getting married. The guy asked her eleven years ago, and now he was marrying her. I said to him, 'What took you so long?' That's the same thing with the Red Sox: what took you so long? You think about it, though, eighty-six years wasn't long at all in geological terms.

"So the bar was half-filled with Red Sox fans, half-filled with Yankees fans. As the game went on, you could see the Yankee fans get smaller and smaller, just shrivel up like a testicle on a cold day. It was a sight to see."

The fourth game of the World Series?

"I was in a bar in Sedona, Arizona," Bill Lee says. "I was there for the fathers and sons tournament. We played six games in four days. Tommy Keefe's son, when the Red Sox won, ripped off all his clothes and jumped in the pool outside the bar. Tommy Keefe was proud. We all were proud. My aunt, Annabelle Lee, was there. She's in the Hall of Fame, played baseball during World War II. Her picture is right next to Jackie Robinson's picture in the Hall of Fame. She was proud of Tommy Keefe's son too.

"There was that beautiful eclipse of the moon that night in Arizona. I stood outside. The moon went into total eclipse at the same time the Red Sox won the World Series. That's all it took: a lunar eclipse and four hurricanes hitting four cities in Florida that begin with 'P'—Pensacola, Fort Pierce, Pasco, and I forget the fourth one. A lunar eclipse and four hurricanes. That was the formula."

Really?

"No, it's all about money," Bill Lee says. "It's always been about money. The New York Yankees, when they won the World Series in 1921, eighty-one of those wins were by pitchers they bought from the Red Sox. It's money. We won it now with a mercenary team the same way the Yankees did, the Marlins did, the Diamondbacks. Everything is mercenaries. It's the Year of the Samurai. Mercenaries are everywhere. If you're a Republican, you pay some kid from Mexico to go die for you in Fallujah. Everything is money.

"If you look, though, at all of those famous Red Sox losses, there's been a managerial blunder behind every one of them. I suppose '46 wasn't so bad, because Dominic DiMaggio got hurt and that other guy had to play center field and Enos Slaughter scored from first. Slaughter was fast. I saw pictures of him run. I met him once. I said, 'How'd you run so fast?' He said, 'You'd run fast too if you had five wives.'"

Any thoughts about your own career come back to you during all of this craziness about the Red Sox?

"I was on a show from Maui, *ESPN Classic* or something, before the last game of the Yankees series," Bill Lee says. "Sean McDonough asked me why I threw a hanging curveball to Tony Perez in the seventh game in '75. I said, *'Because I'm a breaking ball pitcher.'* I heard something in my earpiece during that show that [Boston talk-show host] Eddie Andelman said the Red Sox were never going to win in his lifetime. I said, 'Well, you'd better get your affairs in order and you'd better not go on any long rides with your kids.'

"I told the Yankees fans at the airport the next day that George Steinbrenner was so mad he was going to move the team to the Philippines. He was going to change the name to the Manila Folders." Anything else?

"The Red Sox need me now to keep that team together," Bill Lee says. "A little yoga. Some meditation. You're going to have to have socialism to keep that team together. Get me with them. I'll convince them not to take the money. The Red Sox will be a dynasty, and Massachusetts will secede from the United States. It'll all be great.

"Really, those hitters should think twice about going someplace else. Fenway pads their stats. Garciaparra should have paid to play there, not asked for more money. I said three years ago they should get rid of him. The way he throws he makes all your first basemen look horseshit."

Anything else?

"I'm still pissed about the election," Bill Lee says. "I always knew the stupid and the rich would join together and rule the country."

Thank you.

❖

Bob Wood (retired):

"Tris Speaker was my father's roommate for fifteen years," Bob Wood says. "Speaker was a glorious, great man. He died in 1958 when he was pulling a boat out of the water. Had a heart attack and died right there.

"My dad was kind of laid-back. Speaker was kind of outspoken. Again, a great guy. He played that shallow center field. There were stories that when he came up in 1908 with the Red Sox, Cy Young was still on the team. Cy Young would take him to the outfield and hit fungoes to him by the hour. That was how Speaker learned to play so shallow. If a ball was hit over his head, he'd just run back, turn around, and catch it. I don't think anyone's ever done that as well as he did. They talk about Willie Mays and Joe DiMaggio, well, they better put Tris Speaker in there too. He was as good as anyone who ever played."

Wood is 85 years old, long retired from the health care business. He lives in Keene, New Hampshire. His father was Smokey Joe Wood, who pitched with the Red Sox from 1908 until 1915, when his arm wore out. Smokey Joe then joined former Sox teammate Speaker in Cleveland, where he played the outfield for three more seasons. In 1912 he had a 34–5 record and won three games in the Series for the world champion Red Sox.

Smokey Joe Wood lived to be 95 years old, dying in 1985. Bob Wood would travel with him to various events and met most of the legendary ballplayers from the long ago past.

"The Red Sox had a pretty good dynasty going when my father was playing," the son says. "They won it '03, '04, '11, '12, and '16 and '18. We lived in Pennsylvania after he retired, and players would come to visit. I met Gehrig, Ruth, Ty Cobb. All of them. Ruth was just a big, big boy. He was a grown-up boy.

"Lawrence Ritter was doing that book *The Glory of Their Times*. He came to interview my father. Had a big tape recorder. My father talked, and Ritter left, and my father had second thoughts about the things he said. Mostly about Ruth. He told how the other players called Ruth 'The Big Baboon.' My father called Ritter, and Ritter came back, and they did it all over again. And my father didn't talk about The Big Baboon."

Wood has followed the Red Sox for all of his life. He always thought their problem simply was "they couldn't win the seventh game." He wasn't a believer in any Curse of The Big Baboon.

In the ALCS in 2004 the Red Sox surprised him. They asked him to come down to Fenway to throw out the first ball for the fourth game against the Yankees. They also brought in Bill Carrigan Jr., son of the catcher in the Red Sox's championship battery in 1912. Wood was delighted. He appeared at the designated time, threw his pitch ("I was able to get my arm around and throw the ball, and Bill Jr. was able to catch it"), and watched the first half of the game from a luxury box.

Leaving early to beat the crowd at 85, Wood and his wife listened to the game on the car radio on the ride back to New Hampshire. A little bit over the state line, the station faded and the game disappeared. The Woods went home and went to bed.

"The Red Sox were losing when the game disappeared," Bob Wood says. "I figured they lost. I thought the series was finished and that was that for the season. I said, 'Oh well.' It wasn't until the morning and I looked at the paper and saw that they won. That turned out to be a pretty good surprise."

5. The Story of the Amazing Thread

THE COMPUTER CAMPFIRE HAS BECOME A PLACE FOR Red Sox fans to gather. If 'Nuf Ced McGreevey's saloon at 949 Columbus Avenue in Roxbury was the spot for Boston baseball die-hards to discuss the fortunes and misfortunes of the local nine at the turn of the last century—proprietor M. T. McGreevey acquired his nickname by shouting "'nuf ced" to end all arguments—the Sons of Sam Horn website is the spot at the turn of this century.

Dozens of Sox sites have sprung up, allowing Sox fans to chat about all subjects, good and bad and seldom indifferent, but the Sons of Sam Horn has moved to the front. Started by Eric Christensen, a paper-mill worker in Salem, New York, in 2001 as a spin-off from another site dedicated to another obscure former ballplayer, dickiethon.com, the site became so popular that membership eventually had to be capped off simply to keep discussions manageable and to freeze out the foul mouths and the screamers.

"We didn't want a bunch of idiots pissing in our flower-pot," founder Christensen says. "If you know what I mean."

When the Red Sox rallied back after losing the first three ALCS games in 2004 against the Yankees, the series tied, seventh game approaching, an amazing string of messages began to appear. A teacher in Greenwich, Connecticut, Shaun Kelly, sent the first one, asking the Red Sox to win the seventh game and the Series for a list of people, both former players and his friends. This opened what in the web world is called "a thread": one message after another arrived from around the world asking the Red Sox to "Win It For" various friends and loved ones. The postings piled on, hundreds and hundreds of messages, dedications that shined a deep, deep light into the souls of Red Sox fans.

How much did a World Championship mean? People told how much it meant, eloquently and with passion, using computer aliases that by themselves showed how closely each typist was tied to the story.

Shaun Kelly (English teacher):

"Actually, I first posted something very similar to this year's message about an hour before the seventh game against the Yankees in 2003," Shaun Kelly says. "I've always thought the ghosts of Fenway had nothing to do with Babe Ruth or any of that stuff. The ghosts were our fathers and our grandfathers, our teachers and coaches, the people who passed the game on to us and are no longer around. You go to Fenway and you see the ghosts. That doesn't happen anywhere else, not even Yankee Stadium, because it's been renovated. Fenway, I remember going to a game with my Uncle Seaver, who lived to be ninety-two years old and had seen Babe Ruth pitch many times for the Red Sox. He said, 'I used to sit in section 14,' and there it was, section 14. Right there.

"On the Sons of Sam Horn, there's what we call a game thread. You can post during a game, comment on what is happening, and people will comment back. About an hour before game seven in 2003, I made my post. Maybe thirty people answered, all very interesting, but then Aaron Boone hit that home run and that was it. Everything vanished into the abyss of existentialism.

"When this year rolled around, another seventh game, I posted again. A little different perhaps, but not much. And then the messages started coming. And they didn't stop."

Kelly is such a Red Sox fan that his story was included in the HBO special *The Curse of the Bambino*. He was the one who quit a good job in Jacksonville, Florida, in 1978 because the Red Sox were 14½ games ahead in the AL East and he was convinced they were going to win everything and he didn't want to miss the show. He wound up with a bad job in Boston and a seat in the bleachers when Bucky Dent homered in the one-game playoff to complete the Boston fold. Kelly was the one who compared being a Red Sox fan to being Sisyphus, rolling the big rock up a hill, over and over, only to see it roll back down again. He was the one who took the long walk in Newton after the 1986 finish.

"I was surprised there were so many people out there doing the same thing I was," he says. "It was late. I saw one guy, he had his shirt off and he was shouting, 'I'm free, I'm free, I'll never follow those fuckers again.' I met an old couple and we talked. They said, 'We just wanted to see it happen once in our lifetime.'"

Kelly has worked at the Greenwich Country Day School for the past 18 years. He found that the Sons of Sam Horn board was a way for him to connect with other long-challenged souls. He took the name "jacklamabe65" in honor of the former Sox pitcher who later became his baseball coach at Jacksonville University. The responses to his 2004 "Win It For" post were staggering.

"It was almost voyeuristic to read them," Kelly says. "They're from members, a lot of them, but a lot are not. People who read the board but can't participate are called 'lurkers.' I was getting thirty, forty messages a day from lurkers who wanted to be included. I just kept posting."

Here, with the permission of Kelly and Eric Christensen, is a taste of the thread. The first message from jacklamabe65, posted prior to game seven of the American League Championship Series, is the one that started the progression:

Win it for Johnny Pesky, who deserves to wear a Red Sox uniform in the dugout during the 2004 World Series. Mr. Henry, the trophy needs to be presented first of all to him.

Win it for Bobby Doerr, who, through the sadness of losing his beloved Monica, would love to see his Sox finally defeat New York in Yankee Stadium. Revenge is best served cold.

Win it for Dom DiMaggio, the most loyal and devoted of men. If he hadn't gotten hurt in Game 7 of the '46 Series, Enos Slaughter would never have scored.

Win it for Carl Yastrzemski. While his heart still aches today, may a smile break through his personal storm-cloud this evening. His beloved son, Mike, will show us the way. God speed, number 8.

Win it for Ted Williams, who once said, "If they ever won it, I would feel so damn warm inside."

Win it for Tony Conigliaro, who taught us all the meaning of courage and grit. A day doesn't go by when I don't think of you, number 25.

Win it for Ned Martin, Ken Coleman, and Jim Woods—who provided us with nothing less than the soundtrack to our childhoods.

Win it for Richard Gorman, who followed the team passionately while residing in Queens and the Bronx. He was a master teacher, a supportive friend, and a diehard Red Sox fan.

Most of all, win it for James Lawrence Kelly, 1913–1986. This one's for you, Daddy. You always told me that loyalty and perseverance go hand in hand. Thanks for sharing the best part of you with me.

—jacklamabe65

Just like last year, there will be an empty spot on the couch as I watch game seven.

Dad cheered for the Sox from the age of eight in 1930. He went to games at Fenway with his father and told me about it when he took me to the most glorious stadium on God's green earth.

My father passed away in 2001; which means, of course, that he never saw the Sox win in his lifetime. One of his final moments of clarity was seeing Rivera blow the save and the D-Backs winning the World Series.

That was also his last smile.

I believe my father has been busy lately, along with a lot of other fathers and grandfathers and brothers and sons . . . helping umps see the truth and helping Ortiz lead the way.

That hand of God Curt talked about? It was a legion of dearly departed Sox fans, of which my dad was one.

And so, again this year, there will be that empty spot on the couch . . . reserved for my dad. I can only hope he's sitting there with me.

So please . . . win one for Everett Bentley Baker II (1922–2001).

—TrapperAB

Win it for my Grandpa Harvey (1974) who would rise up from his seat along the RF line in the grandstand and defend the Scotty from the boo birds, even if the Boomer was hitting .170 in 1968.

Win it for that 7 year old kid who fell in love with a game and a ball team that long ago magical summer of 1967. And for that 18 year old kid who sat in the LF grandstand and watched the pop up nestle into the screen on 10/2/78.

Win it for Grace Elizabeth, who will arrive any day now, and be able to say she was alive when the Sox won the Series.

And win it for her Grandparents Norm (1960) and Betty (2000) who raised their son in such a way that he could weep unashamedly at the signs of loyalty, love, affection and warmth that are contained herein.

And most of all, win it for yourselves, who deserve
this more than anything else in the world; who persevered and fought and refused to quit.

—Norm Siebern

Win it for Ack, my Grandfather who, in 1986 with the
Sox having the game sewed up with two outs and two
strikes and a two run lead in the tenth, told me and my
brother, "I've never seen a Sox Championship, your father has never seen a Sox Championship, now you will
see one," only to have his heart ripped out and to walk to
the other room without a word. He was as die hard as
they come, he lived through the hard New England winters with the hope of what the Sox would bring the next
summer. He passed away in 2001 in the same room he
watched game 6 in 1986. Maybe he can pull some strings
tonight!

—Carl Everett's Therapist

Win it for Nana Greeney. My dad was born in the
Bronx in 1943 and was saved a life of Yankeedom by
Nana Greeney, the toughest, roughest, kindest-hearted
crusty old Irish Brooklyn Dodger fan of the bunch. She
hated the Yankees like the Catholics hated Cromwell,
and she brought my Dad up right. There but for the
grace of God, and all. . . . My dad said once, "I don't remember Nana Greeney crying when my Grandfather
died, but I know she cried tears of joy when the Dodgers
finally won the World Series." Somewhere up there I
know she's pulling for the BoSox.

And win it for my Dad. Born a Brooklyn Dodger fan
and soon abandoned, he went to Vietnam, came back,
went to law school in Boston and met this beautiful
woman in class. They fell in love playing footsie during
the '75 World Series and the rest is history. He's 60, so he's
not old, but he's no younger than all the other 60-year-
olds who have come and gone without seeing them win it
all.

This is the year. I believe.

Edit: And this year I want to go without making that
call to Dad saying "I thought they had it this year. I really
thought they had it." Just once I want to laugh with him,
over the phone or in person, and pour champagne and
rejoice.

—Old Fart Tree

Win it for my son James who was born on September 30. He is the cutest kid in the world and the
Sox are 6–0 when he watches the game on his father's
lap. Unfortunately James has Down's Syndrome. My
wife and I probably would've terminated the preg-
nancy had we done an amnio and learned this, but
because of the trouble we had conceiving and the fact
that James had a twin that did not survive, the doctors suggested against it. He is truly a special kid and
he deserves to grow up knowing that the joy and
strength he has brought us may somehow magically
have helped the Sox win. And yes, he will be on my
lap tonight.

—Clears Cleaver

Win it for my grandfather, born right after the
Sox won in 1918, and then passed away a week after
the loss in '86, devastated and heartbroken at the Sox
loss.

Win it so I can go down with a Guinness, and drink
one with him at the gravesite. Win so I can cry tears I've
never cried.

Win it for Red Sox fans who are soldiers overseas who
need something to hold onto.

Win it for Red Sox nation. The hurt will go away. The
pain stops. Tonight the heavens open, and it is good.

Love you and miss you gramps, this one's for you. And
all of the rest of the family of this board watching with ya
tonight.

—DaveJustice

These messages were posted after the Red Sox beat the
Yankees:

There was a point during this season that was very,
very tough. But I came here, read the Bandwagon thread
and was uplifted by the depth and breadth of your faith.
It was at that time the best thing we were reading anywhere.

These guys—I'm so proud of them—refused to lose
for the faithful this week. I'm proud of everyone who refused to get off this bandwagon.

—John W. Henry (owner of the Boston Red Sox)

John Kiley played "The Hallelujah Chorus" in heaven

last evening. Sherm Feller made the following announce-
ment, "Ladies and gentlemen, boys and girls, the 2004
American League Champions, the Boston Red Sox."

—jacklamabe65

These messages were posted before and during the
World Series:

Win it for my Grandfather, John Steven McDonough.

Grandpa was born in Boston in 1927 and followed the
Sox through the good and bad times, which were unfortunately mostly bad for him.

My earliest memories of the Red Sox are of sitting in
the Grandstand with my Grandpa, cheering for Pudge
Fisk while he had himself another beer. It was a scene
that would be repeated quite often through my childhood.

I remember the pain of watching the 86 series with
him, and aside from the night my Grandma had a mas-
sive, paralyzing stroke, it's the only other time I can remember him crying.

Although I live in Tampa, FL now, I visited my
grandfather in the Summer of 2000. To try and repay
him for everything he'd ever done for me, I took him to
Fenway Park for a game. 10th row Field Box, 3rd base
line. He was an old man at this point, 72, and he struggled to shuffle up the steep ramp into the stadium. But
when his eyes met the grass of Fenway's pristine field,

they lit up. I swear he immediately looked 20 years younger. We watched Pedro Martinez out duel James Baldwin and the White Sox 1–0, and Pedro struck out 15. He leaned to me near the end of the game and told me that these were the best seats he'd ever had in his life for a Red Sox game.

As we exited Fenway, me slowing down to allow him to shuffle at his own pace, we talked about his childhood, and what it was like growing up in Boston and being a Sox fan for so long. When he got winded, we would sit on T Station benches and just talk until he felt strong enough to get to the car. It was a day I'll never forget, because as he shared the stories of the Sox and his life, it was the first time I ever felt his mortality.

Two months later, he died of stomach cancer, never seeing the Red Sox win it all.

Please, just win this for Grandpa. Although I've cried tears of mourning for him numerous times since his passing, sometimes waking up in the night after having a particularly sad, vivid dream of him, I know that the day is soon coming where I can visit his grave with my little boy and tell him all about his Great-Grandpa, about Loyalty, about Love, and about what it truly means to be a Sox fan like my Grandpa was . . . to be a champion 1000 times over and hopefully one day get to taste the real thing.

—justify73

This is for my grandpa.

Edward Hagerty, of East Providence, R.I., and later
Bridgeport, CT, then Monroe, CT.

1912–1995. He was just a lad when they won it for
the last time, but I know Grandpa Ed is looking
down on me, smiling, knowing his beloved Red Sox
(only through his efforts, and I mean EFFORTS, did
a young Fairfield County boy named Larry root for
the Red Sox, not the Yankees) have finally won the
World Series.

We brought out a picture of him and turned it toward the TV. He got a sip of champagne. If I could,
I'd fly back tomorrow and stick a big fat Red Sox flag
next to his gravestone.

—Spaceman's Bong

I have avoided posting here since the playoffs started
several weeks ago. My sister, who lived in Montana with
my family, was killed by a drunk driver on Sept. 28. She
was on her way home from work, and a woman, with a
previous DUI conviction, almost ran another guy off a
road, then flipped a u—turn and took my sister out head
on at 70 mph. It was 4 days before my sister's 30th birthday and 6 days before my Dad's.

None of my family members were home except for my
mother when she received the news. The phone call I received from her was the most devastating and traumatic
phone call ever, and will be burned into my head for the
rest of my life. My life and my family's has been an upside
down hell since then. I do not live at home, and with no
family around, things have been difficult.

I watched the LDS and LCS thinking that my sister was watching and perhaps influencing or orchestrating things. I refused to post here because I did not want to bum others out. I kept to myself. The MFY winning only occurred because my brother is an MFY fan, I thought. She wanted him to be happy and for me to enjoy a win all the more. Still, I doubted the Sox along with many other things because of the depression I am still in.

By Game 6 many friends and family members were calling me speaking of divine intervention, destiny and signs. When the Sox clinched last night, I broke down and wept for a good 10 minutes or more. My sister knew of the love and devotion I have for the Sox. She was with me in 86 watching Game 6 on television. I remember her coloring in her color book and her freaking out on me as I threw the crayons across the room as the game slipped away. Last night, I felt she was with me again.

I hope the Sox win for her, or with her, or whatever the case may be. All I know is that this post season will always be bittersweet and will be something I will remember for the rest of my life.

—Robinson Checo

Win it for the young man who burst into tears and almost lost all hope in life on the evening of October 21, 2003.

—A lurker

Win it for my brother, who worked on the 94th
floor of the North Tower, and who died on September
11th, 2001. He used to look out the window and stick
his tongue out in the direction of the Bronx. Above
his desk, he had a framed picture of Fenway with two
baseball cards scotch-taped to the bottom: Reggie
Smith and Pudge Fisk—his two favorite Sox players
growing up. Many times when he worked, he would
proudly wear his Sox hat. I sometimes think that after
the plane hit, he put his Sox hat on for the last time.

—PUDGEcanCATCH

Win it for my Dad, who idolized Ted Williams
growing up in his New Jersey neighborhood even
though all the other kids rooted for Joe DiMaggio.
Who would sit outside on the deck of our NJ home
and fight through the static to get WTIC out of
Hartford, and who made his kids Sox fans in the heart
of Yankee country. He's 70 now, has the baseball package on his TV instead of an old radio, but still watches
every pitch of every game.

For my mother, who doesn't understand baseball
one lick, but understands the passion the men in her
life have for the Red Sox all too well.

For my brother, who works in NYC and endured
more taunts and jeers than I could have ever put up
with after Game 7 last year.

For my 7 year old nephew, who had to unlearn his foot
tapping wiffleball ways when his favorite player was
traded earlier this year, and who still doesn't understand

why the other kids in his NJ first grade class taunt him with "Red Sox suck!"—May he have the last laugh this year.

For my pregnant wife, who somehow jumped up and down higher than me when her favorite player broke out of his slump and hit a grand slam in Game 7.

And finally, for my unborn child, who I can someday tell was watching along with us when the Sox finally won it, and who will grow up in a world where the words "Red Sox" and "Cursed" won't be synonymous.

—Cypher74

Win it for my father, Rick Anderson Sr. (1945–1994). My Dad lived for the Red Sox. I was his youngest daughter and since my brother didn't come along until seven years after me, I guess my Dad got scared he might not get a son, so he decided to make sure he instilled his love of the game into one of us. It worked. Once my brother came along, it became double the fun for my Dad.

My Dad did it right, too—by the time I was nine years old, he had already taken me to Cooperstown and spring training. He took me out of school on Opening Days—and even caught a foul ball for me one year! He took me out of school when Roger Clemens had his book signing (I adored Clemens and still to this day I proudly stand behind him, Bill Simmons, be damned! :-).) He taught me about everything in Fenway, from the retired numbers to the Morse code. And he succeeded in his goal—I live and die by this team and I wouldn't trade it for anything in the world.

In the ten years that my Dad has been gone, not a day goes by that I don't think of him and miss him terribly. But I can honestly say that I have never wished so badly that he was here more than I do right now. My God, how he would love this team. Not just for what they have done, but for how they have done it. With heart, with class, and with sheer joy. Just the way it's supposed to be.

After Game 2 of the ALCS, I had a dream about my Dad. I dreamt that I met him at Fenway for a game. We got there early, so early that we were virtually the only ones in the park. We were sitting in the seats that were our very first season tickets, from when I was a child. He was wearing a Red Sox t-shirt, and when I walked up the ramp to our seats and saw him, sitting there all alone in the empty park, he simply smiled and hugged me. I know that it was his way of letting me know that he is here and he is watching. And he is very, very happy.

We still have my Dad's season tickets, so I will be at Game 2 on Sunday night. And I know my Dad will be there with me. Please, win this for him.

—A Sox lurker

Win it for my Dad, a US Foreign Service man and a Sox fan who introduced me to the team in 1961. He died in an airplane accident in the Philippines in September 1976, before his time at age 49. His last World Series experience was huddling with 2 friends around a short wave radio in Lima, Peru, cursing first the bad reception on Voice of America and then the outcome of Game 7 versus the Reds.

Win it for my friend and longtime business partner Angus Mountain, a lifelong Sox fan from Dover-Foxcroft, Maine who passed away from liver cancer this past May at age 50. Last September, a group of his buddies flew with Angus to his last Sox game, a day trip to Camden Yards, where he saw Pedro shut out the Orioles.

Also, win it for all of the Sox heroes who couldn't quite get there, including:

—Johnny, Dom, Bob, and Ted.

—Jim Lonborg, who gave it his all on 2 days rest in Game 7.

—El Tiante, who threw 160 pitches in Game 4 back in '75.

—Bernie Carbo, who brought us back from the abyss in Game 6.

—The '78 team, for winning 8 straight to force the playoff game.

—RemDawg, who should have had an inside the park home run. I still can't believe Piniella blindly snagged that ball.

—Steamer, who really wanted the ball in the 10th inning of Game 6, and who did his part.

—Tudor Fever

Win it for Chris Phelan who was killed by a drunk driver on 1/18/00 at the age of 29. He was a beloved third grade teacher, son, brother, uncle and knowledgeable Sox fan.

We have both Red Sox and Yankee fans at our school and had great fun discussing the games with Chris. (Some days the kids would benefit with extended recess when we got carried away with our baseball talk.)

I'm sure his parents, brothers and sister were celebrating with a heavy heart after Wednesday's win.

I pumped my fists towards the sky to celebrate with Chris that night . . . I have to believe he had something to do with that historic come back.

—SoxGal15

I'm a SOSH lurker, also a teacher of English and History, also a lifelong citizen of RSN, from a few miles away from your birthplace, hoping you'll have a moment to post this for me vicariously.

Win this one for my old English professor, Bart Giamatti. When he was offered the presidency of Yale, he told the college newspaper, "All I ever wanted to be president of was the American League." Then he became the president of the other league, and in '86 he had to grit his teeth and pretend to be happy as the Mets took home the trophy, though everyone who knew him knew his heart was breaking as much as any of ours. He wrote about his love of the game (which meant his love of the Sox) as passionately as anybody, which made it doubly satisfying that he got to be the one to mete out justice to the pernicious Rose—even though doing so killed him.

And for Grampa Dan, born six months before the last championship. He took my older brother and me to our first game when we were six and five, probably too young to know what was going on, but he wanted us to see Ted Williams once before he retired. On that infamous Saturday night in October '86 when Schiraldi batted (Schiraldi batted!!!) while Baylor, Stapleton, and Greenwell languished on the bench, I called him in the tenth inning to be sure he was still up and would be able to see the astonishing thing that was about to happen. Red Sox fatalist that he was, he wondered if I had jinxed them by doing anything remotely close to celebrating before it was over. I think he went to his death two and a half years later at least partly blaming me as much as McNamara and Schiraldi for the awful turn of events. (We never blamed Buckner. Nobody dast blame this man.)

Last October, as Boone's blast sailed out of Yankee Stadium, I put my hand on the slumped shoulder of the twelve-year-old grandson he never knew—my son—and channeled what must have been his words as much as mine: "Now you know what it means to be a Red Sox fan. Welcome to my world." But maybe I was wrong. As of right now, the Yankees have won no more championships in the twenty-first century than the Red Sox have—and only one of them still has a chance to do so this year.

Some morning next week, in the hours just after dawn, the cemeteries all over RSN will be filled with middle-aged men, standing by ancestral graves marked (whatever the headstone) with the same bronze veterans' plaques at the foot—First Sergeant, Staff Sergeant, PFC, served some range of years beginning with a high school graduation and ending with 1945. We will be reading aloud from tear-stained newspapers, sharing our first too-early libation of the day. (A Gansett? A Ballantine Ale?) We will be drinking to Cabrera's defense, Foulke's grit, Damon's grace, Ortiz's incredible sense of timing. MAYBE we'll even have a reason to toast Manny. We will be waving the bloody sock—thanking God and Theo for sending us Schilling, on whom all our hopes rested, and did not rest in vain. Remembering all those who came so close but did not get there, like Yaz and Lonborg and Boomer and Rico and Hawk and Tiant and Dewey and Jim Ed and Fisk and Mo and even Nomar. Remembering all those who did not live to see us get there, like Ted and Tony C and Grampa Dan. The clock will be unwinding, the pages will be flying off the calendar, the earth will tilt slightly on its axis. I will be there. My brothers will be there. Get there early. It's going to be crowded.

—A Red Sox Lurker

Win it for longtime SoSHer RomeroRomine, who is currently working as a civilian at a military compound in Iraq. P&G just hasn't been the same since you went over there, my friend. We will keep you in our thoughts and prayers.

Thank you for serving our country so nobly.

—jacklamabe65

Win it for my dad who used to listen to the radio in

the kitchen when I'd go to games at Fenway just so we'd
have something to talk about when I came home, and
whose memory has betrayed him to the point where he
doesn't automatically recognize the faces of the people
who love him.

Win it for my late Uncle Tom Griffin who took me
to my first game in '77 v. the Orioles and my late cousin
Jim Collins who brought me to several games there-
after.

Win it for Victoria Snelgrove and her friends and
family, and for the Boston police officer who must feel
awful about causing her death.

Win it for Crash Bartash who we woke up from a
drunken stupor with two outs to go in Game 6 in '86 just
so he could witness the Red Sox winning the World Series, and who I last saw wandering off shirtless and de-
spondent into the night.

Win it for all of us because it has been a long 18 years
since we had our last chance.

—Yazlooksupanditsgone

Win it for my Pa. He died on my 16th birthday in
1997—he'd been born in 1919, loved thumbing his
nose at the people who damned Ted Williams, took
his wife—my grandmother—to Fenway to see the
sights. He loved Ted not just because he was such a
great ballplayer, and because he was his own man—he
loved him because he and Ted were both excellent pi-
lots in WWII, they were contemporaries, nearly the
same age, in the prime of life. Proud Air Force men

through and through. I have more Ted Williams
books with his specter than nearly every other kind of
book combined. When he'd coach me to hit for Little
League, he'd say, "Do this—this is what Ted Williams
did, Timothy."

He was quiet, small—but remarkably commanding.
Everyone in my family tells about how he would show
up early to Fenway for batting practice, slowly slide his
way to the edge of the seats, make inevitable eye contact
with a Sox player and call him over with a wave of his
hand.

And the multimillion dollar athlete would come.
George Scott, Carl Yastrzemski, Carlton Fisk, Bruce
Hurst, Jim Lonborg, Fred Lynn. My Pa would put an
arm around their necks and tell them how much he and
the city loved them. The last guy he did it with was Mo
Vaughn, a player he literally fell in love with. He never
got too high on the Red Sox, and we never saw him get
too low. In '86, my mother called him from Rhode Island
where she and my dad were vacationing. My dad was
devastated.

"Dad," she said to my grandpa, "are you OK? They did
it again, didn't they?"

"Yeah, they did, Mae. They did."

And there he was next April, yearbook in hand, sitting
back in his chair, idly fixing a VCR remote or the wiring
in a lamp, listening to the game on the radio and watching it on TV. Never too high, never too low, but always
loved them to absolute death.

Baseball is in my genes because of my grandfather—

he even played low A ball for the Brooklyn Dodgers at one point. He gave it to me, so win one for him.

—JohntheBaptist

I have read every single response in that thread and cried my eyes out numerous times. It describes the heart and soul of what it means to be a Red Sox fan. I wished I had a way to add. Glad I do now. Thanks for coming here and starting a thread for us to post in.

Win it for my Nonna. Born in October of 1917, she's lived her entire life in Medford or Somerville and yet she's never been to Fenway Park. Mostly crippled and deaf now, she'll probably never make it. Doesn't matter to her. She still watches the game every single night and roots for the Sox.

Win it for my dad, who's loved this team since he was born in 1951. And stayed with them through 1967, 1975, 1978, 1986 and all those other years. He's been going through hell for the past 3 and half years. He lost his job then and my parents have struggled to make a go of it with their own small business. I've had to watch them lose their dream house, completely powerless to do any-thing but help pack boxes. It has been a never-ending nightmare. Baseball is his distraction. I just want him to have something to smile about. There's nothing else I can do. Except to pray for a win.

—Red Sox Nation Dcaf

Please win it for my father, who adopted the Red Sox because I did. We fought over my jerseys and shirts and watched games together since I (well, *we*) joined Red Sox Nation when I was 12. He was as upset as I was when Roger left, because he knew Roger was the reason I'd joined up with the team. He thought it was the coolest thing in the world when I met Yaz, Bobby Doerr, Mo and Ellis. He called me when I was away at University to tell me about stuff during the off-season when everyone at school was worried over our University basketball team. He joined me in my frustration year after year, even though he grew weaker with illness.

Daddy died of brain cancer in April. One of the last things I told him was, "You gotta tell Ted Williams 'hello' for me." I know he isn't physically here with me, but I also know that he *is* here with me, and I can almost hear him laughing with Teddy Ballgame about that amazing ALCS.

Whether or not we win the series, this is hugely emotional because it's the first time I will be watching without my father next to me. Our team being in it is completely brilliant.

For all of the fans who lived and didn't see the team win whilst here, please win, fellas. They are all up there with the angels rooting for you.

—Leesha

Win it for my Dad, on whose lap I sat on those long-ago weekend afternoons. We'd be inside on a beautiful summer day. The Sox game on TV, my Dad with a sandwich and a 'Gansett, the distant buzz of a neighbor's lawnmower and smell of fresh-cut grass became the image of summer for me. . . . He got me started with this addiction and took me to my first games in the late 60's. . . .

Win it for Sister Mary Bruce, who infected an entire 5th grade class with Sox fever in '67, going so far as dragging a TV set into class to let us catch parts of the playoff games and having us imitate the players when we played kickball at gym. . . .

Win it for my dear departed Uncle Chet, who lived in Pittsfield and took my cousins and myself to see the AAA Red Sox there in long-ago summers, where we were able to talk to players and get autographs and really get up close and personal to the game.

—Southpaw67

I'd like to add my father to the list as well. He has been a steady and loyal Sox fan for nearly 60 years through many difficult personal battles, not the least of which was the passing of my sister in 1983. For his 50th birthday (a few years later), my mother and I sent him to the Red Sox Fantasy Camp in Florida. He spent hours with Bobby Doerr, Luis Tiant, Bernie Carbo, Dick Radatz, and many others. He talks to this day about roping a double off El Tiante and paying the price of hours in the trainer's room as a result (pulled muscles he didn't know he had). No matter how down he may be at anytime (and he's never been the same since her death), I'm always able to cheer him up by asking about the night he spent at the bar with Teddy Ballgame. He bought the Splinter a few Old Grandad's and was honored with a conversation that included the art of hitting as well as a few lectures on other topics. Ted wouldn't sign a ball for him, but said he would for my mom. Dad always spoke so highly of him that I regret never having had the opportunity to meet him myself. Dad gave me the ball a few years back with the warning that I had better never sell it. I wouldn't care if someone offered me a thousand dollars, its worth so much more to me because of how much it means to him.

I grew up a Yaz fan and when dad's co-workers presented him with an autographed Yaz bat at his retirement, he immediately gave it to me. My favorite memory as a kid comes from the day that he and I (along with my uncle and cousin) took the train into Boston for a day at Fenway. Dad got us seats in the left field corner so that I could see Yaz up close and personal. I'll also never forget the night he sat outside Fenway park after sitting through a rainy doubleheader of losses while I waited for Yaz to walk out to his car. My sister had passed away recently and I'm sure that sitting in the car in the rain after those two tough losses so that I could get Yaz's autograph was pretty low on his list of things to do, but he did it for me and our love of the Sox.

That's how it is with the two of us. I'm still trying to get World Series tickets and I don't care if I have to drive to Missouri or Massachusetts, I'm determined to give him the gift of seeing them live in the WS. The Red Sox have become more than a bond between us, they transcend so many things.

As much as I want to see a World Championship, it

just won't be the same if it doesn't happen in my dad's lifetime. I'm certain that there are many of you out there that know exactly what I mean.

—Yaz4Ever

My story is hardly unique, and in some ways eerily similar to some things I have read, but it means a lot to me, because its mine, and if you could post it that would be great.

I was born in Boston in 1986, the year of Buckner. In our small apartment my mom would nurse me right next to the radio (we didn't have a TV). You could say I was born a Sox fan. When the ball went through Buckner's legs, my mom got so unhappy I started to cry. When the Mets won, my mom said I cried harder than I ever have in my whole life since.

Growing up, my dad would take me to as many Sox games a year as money and time would allow for. He was working a ton at that time, and we didn't exactly have money, but we still went to at least 4 games a year. My great uncle Manny (yeah, I know it's a coincidence, his real name was Emanuel, just like my dad) would often come along, the only other family member in Boston at the time. He was obsessed with Ted Williams, and through my mediocre years in Little League his advice to me was always, always, "do it like Teddy." I never could, but he didn't care. He's dead now, died in 2002 without ever seeing the Sox win the World Series.

When we moved out of Boston I think I missed the Sox more than I did anything else. In New Jersey I found myself adrift in a sea of Yankees fans, the source of more fights during recess than I can count.

Which was, in a way, how I met my best friend. The only other Boston fan in my school, she and I banded together at first out only through Baseball, and we later became inseparable. Her dad and mine met up, became great friends, and each year we would take a trip up to Boston to see the Sox at Fenway (it's just not the same anywhere else).

On 9/11, my best friend's father went into the WTC. He was a cop, he went in there to save people, and in his wallet he had a picture of his daughter, his wife, and of Reggie Smith, his favorite Sox player. He didn't come out, and the following year was heartbreaking, not just for my loss of one of the best men I ever knew growing up, but to see what his loss did to my best friend.

I hadn't gotten into a fight since I was 12. But after Game 7 of the 2003 ALCS, I walked into school to find a guy I knew chanting "1918" and "Red Sox suck" over and over to my best friend. I've never hit anyone that hard in my entire life. My hand ached for a day afterwards. I nearly got suspended for that, nearly lost my scholarship and my admission to NYU, but I would do the exact same thing over again. Without hesitation.

So this is much more than a game for me. This is my parents' entire life of heartbreaking loss after heartbreaking loss. This is my great uncle Manny never seeing his fondest dream come true. This is my best friend's dad and his sacrifice and his love of the team. This is the most important friendship I have ever had.

A win this year will not wipe that all away. But it
doesn't need to. My great uncle, my parents, my best
friend's dad, my best friend and I. We've never asked to
erase history, to dismiss it. All we've ever wanted is one
Sox world championship.

—Literally Exaggerated

Win it for my aunt, God rest her soul, who at her funeral, the priest said, "She was a woman of great faith.
She believed she'd see a Red Sox championship in her
lifetime."

—Captain Laddie

Win it for Lou Thompkins, those of you fortunate
enough to know who he is will fully understand. For
those of you who don't, Google his name. There is an entire little league organization named after him here in
Eastern Massachusetts, and it is my firm belief that he
has kept more young kids out of trouble in the summer
time than anyone anywhere has done voluntarily. Coach
Thompkins suffered a terrible accident years ago, and his
health was failing, last I had heard. Nobody deserves a
win like he does. . . .

Win it for my father who tirelessly taught me the
game that I came to love. The man who coached little
league teams in a town which would not let you coach
your own children, just so he could keep an eye on his
kid's friends and make sure they didn't get into trouble.
The man who has given up on this team so many times,
but has fallen in love with them so many more times

than that. The man who can distinguish between a .225 hitter who runs through walls and .350 hitter that is a prima donna and would take the lesser hitter every day and twice on Sundays. The man who has passed his love for this game to me for all the right reasons. The man who let me stay home from school after the 1986 series (I was 11) so we could practice grounders and take our minds off the Sox together.

Thanks Dad, and I hope we get to see them win this one together. . . .

—Deathofthebambino

When I was riding in on the Green Line for Game 1 of the World Series—yes, I still park at Woodland, our old stop, because I am inherently superstitious—a young man with red-rimmed eyes and a small travel bag rode in with me. He was wearing a Sox hat and was obviously trying to stay awake.

"Where did you come from to see this game?" I finally asked him after talking about whether Wake's knuckleball would flutter successfully in such frigid conditions.

"Guam," he smiled. "I work as a bond trader there, but I am originally from Tolland, Connecticut. The second the Sox clinched against the Yankees, I made a reservation."

"Do you have tickets?" I asked.

"No," he replied. "I just had to be in Boston when they played in the World Series. I have hotel reservations at the Sonesta for this weekend and next weekend. I am returning to the Pacific a week from Wednesday. I have to be at the parade if there is one."

Win it for the Sox fan from Guam.

—jacklamabe65

Win it for my brother, Johnny, who left Boston in 1944 for the South Pacific, a Red Sox hat adorning his head. He was a nineteen year old kid who loved five things—his country, his family, the Red Sox, Fenway Park, and Ted Williams. He lost his life at a hellhole called Okinawa.

There hasn't been a single day that hasn't gone by when I don't think of him.

This one's for you, JB.

—Tedsondeck

My grandfather (1907–1997) who in his younger days used to go to the games and as he got older still watched on TV, always adding his own commentary. He is smiling down on us now.

All of us who have logged more hours sleeping on Landsdowne St. these past few weekends than we have in our beds. The sweet reward was being able to witness the energy inside the park during this great run and have amazing stories to share.

All the kids who are up way past their bedtimes and the teachers who are so patient with them in school.

All of us who believe in a higher power, in ourselves and in our team.

All of us who have achieved goals that others thought

were impossible, who have persevered in the face of adversity.

—SoxGal

The Mekong Delta is a long way from Boston. During the summer of 1969, I found myself as a private in the army, fighting in a war that was becoming increasingly unpopular at home. While I was very homesick for Boston, a fellow private named Kevin, born and raised in the Boston area, kept my spirits up. We used to listen to the radio after the hell of patrol. There was one song by Neil Diamond that we used to love listening to in the outskirts of the jungle. We would scream it out at the top of our lungs. The girl in the song was the girl of our dreams! Kevin was a big Sox fan. He especially loved The Boomer. He got Agent Orange and began to fade away in the early eighties. The war killed him in the end. I attended a Sox game against the White Sox this past August. It was cold as hell for a summer afternoon, and the Sox lost in a disappointing fashion. Still, in the bottom of the eighth inning, I began to hear the strains of the song that Kevin and I had sung so well so long ago back in Nam—"Sweet Caroline." Jesus, Kevin's favorite, playing at Fenway. The tears are flowing now as I write this. Win it for Kevin. Win it for "Sweet Caroline."

—Sargeiswaiting

Eight hours after the Red Sox won the World Series, Shaun Kelly ended the thread with this post:

I imagine that many of you woke up your precious children—and held them in front of your television sets—so that they could actually bear witness to the undeniable fact that the impossible is just not a dream.

I imagine that tears began to run down your cheeks as you remembered your grandfathers, your dads and moms, your kid sisters, your first baseball coach, the father who lived next door who taught you how to bat like Tony C.

I imagine that some of you quietly turned off your television sets and headed for the local cemetery so that you could toast one with a beloved relative who had lived—and died—a Red Sox fan.

In the end, Red Sox Nation, this improbable victory surely brought tears and smiles together as close as they can ever be. Like most of you, a kaleidoscope of emotions and thoughts swirled in my mind.

Not long after the final out, I suddenly remembered the elderly man I ran across during a power walk around Newton following Game Six of the 1986 World Series. When he saw me through the early morning mist, utterly dejected, helpless, in the throes of abject pathos, he stopped me and whispered, "Son, this is the darkest day in this town since Jack Kennedy was shot."

He would assuredly agree with me now that this is the happiest day in this town since V.E. Day.

I also thought of my old neighbor from Wellesley, Mr. Jim Lakis, a passionate Red Sox fan for more than fifty years. If you walked by Mr. Lakis's house the day after Game Six back in '86, you would have observed a shattered television in the trash, a baseball bat lodged right through the screen. When I ran across Mrs. Lakis three weeks later at the local Star Market, she burst into tears. "We will never see it, will we, Shaunie," she cried.

While Mr. Lakis died five years ago, Mrs. Lakis did finally see her Sox win the whole damn thing a few hours ago.

In the end, people talk about all the ghosts Red Sox fans live with, but they have it all wrong. It isn't the ghost of Babe Ruth or Bill Buckner or all the names associated with a curse that never really existed. Instead, it is the ghosts we can still see when we walk into Fenway Park. It's our fathers and our mothers and our grandparents. It's our next-door neighbors and our baseball coaches and our aunts. Those are the ghosts that matter to us. Those are the ghosts we see, huddled together, watching their team and the game so intently.

Fans of any team can say this to some extent because life is about sorrow and joy. But it's a little different for Red Sox fans because we're still going to the same ballpark that our parents and grandparents went to. We don't have to imagine them sitting there—we can literally see them as they were.

And then there's commonality of disappointment, of waiting for something that never comes. We all have relatives who died waiting for the Red Sox to win. We all have relatives who wonder how many years they have left. That has now been all put to rest.

For those of us who have followed the Sox for over forty years, the victory marks both a beginning—and an end. While we have made peace with all of our Sox relatives and friends who have passed on over the years, there was always a little unfinished business between us—and them. Now, with this incomparable victory, that too is complete.

And so, after all of these years, we can finally have a clean goodbye to our beloved departed. That is why so many tears were shed in living rooms all over New England and beyond as the World Series trophy was presented to a most heroic and deserving team.

For years, I often wondered how I would react when the Red Sox won a World Series victory. Now I can report my response.

Yes, when the Sox won, I fervently rejoiced with a passion that surprised even me. But later, much later, I went outside. For a long time, I just looked at the moon.

This has been a helluva thread. Thanks for sharing the best part of you with me.

All the best.

Shaun Kelly
aka jacklamabe65

6. The Fan Story

THERE IS NO TYPICAL RED SOX FAN. THE FOLLOWERS of the fortunes, misfortunes, deeds, and misdeeds of the baseball team from Boston are often painted with certain characteristics, deemed as masochistic folk who love to be knocked down and still get up. Maybe there is truth to this for some fan in Kansas who picks the Red Sox out of a hat filled with options, deciding on the plucky underdog, but most Sox fans have stumbled into their love affair.

They have become partners with this team by chance, not choice. They have developed affection for the grown children of Yawkey Way through the years, but sometimes both understanding and patience have been tested. It has been a marriage not of convenience but of hope.

Hope probably has been the one constant for everyone.

❖

Sister Mary Rose (nun):
"I prayed for the Red Sox always in my general prayers this year," Sister Mary Rose of the Cloistered Sisters of the Precious Blood says. "But when they needed more, I prayed

harder. I said, 'Dear Lord, strike this one out.' Or something like that. I was on my knees for most of those games in the playoffs."

Cloistered now for 50 years—this is her jubilee year—Sister Mary Rose left the outside world while Ted Williams was playing for the Red Sox. He had just returned from the Korean War. Jackie Jensen and Jimmy Piersall were with him in the outfield. Mel Parnell was on the mound. Sister Mary Rose remembers seeing Williams on the black-and-white television screen in her dance instructor's studio in Haverhill.

The Red Sox mostly have been a radio comfort for her for these 50 years. There is a television set now at the Monastery of the Precious Blood in Manchester, New Hampshire, but it is only used for "special events." Every now and then one of those "special events" might be a ball game, and Sister Mary Rose will watch a couple of innings, just to put faces with the names, but then will return to her radio.

She is 71 years old. Her entire adult life has been played to a quiet, contemplative background.

"I was very active as a girl," she says. "I was a cheerleader, majorette, captain of the basketball team, softball pitcher, and roller-skating champion. I never thought about going into the convent.

"Just before my senior year at West High in Manchester, my dance teacher in Haverhill had a problem and asked me to run her studio for a year. That meant I had to finish school in Haverhill and they said I would have to pay an out-of-state tuition. I wound up going to St. James Senior

High School for my last year. That was where I first heard the call.

"I held back for two years, just to make sure, and then I joined the order. I was twenty years old. I went into the monastery and didn't come out for twenty-three years, when I attended a funeral. I was amazed, most of all, by what had happened to the roads. They were all these two-lane roads, replacing all the simple roads I had known."

She travels more often outside the monastery now, restrictions slightly lifted because doctors and dentists and other services no longer will come to the facility on Bridge Street. Her basic life, though, is in the same place it has been for the past 50 years. She is awake at 5:30 A.M. for a day filled with prayer and work. Twenty-eight nuns live in the monastery, "twenty-seven of them Red Sox fans, one Yankee." Baseball is a routine subject of conversation.

"There were a lot of prayers for the Red Sox here," Sister Mary Rose says. "The colors of our habits are red and white, same as the team."

The disappointments of the past never shook her faith. Other people were praying in other places for other results. That was all. Doesn't Yankees manager Joe Torre have a sister who is a nun? God can't grant all wishes at all times. Sometimes the results take a while.

Sister Mary Rose was in her room for the final game from St. Louis, same as always, listening to the radio describe the final moments. She was on her knees, same as always. Her celebration, like her life, was quiet. She had a feeling of great satisfaction. The public celebration was the next day.

"Someone brought us a cake," Sister Mary Rose says. "It was very good."

❖

Larry Ronan (doctor):

"I wore my Red Sox hat in Baghdad," Dr. Larry Ronan says. "I was there with a group of doctors attached to the Eighty-second Airborne. We were helping, trying to set up some things with Iraqi doctors. It was just that small time between the war and what is going on now, the time before the suicide bombers. That stuff was just starting.

"I'd be wearing my hat and these soldiers, these kids, would come up to me. 'You like the Red Sox? Are you from Boston? I'm from Worcester.' We would stand there in the Green Zone and talk about the Red Sox. It would happen all day. There were thousands of troops there.

"Here are these kids, don't know what's going to happen next, could get their heads blown off in half an hour, and they wanted to talk about the Red Sox. That shows how strong the affection is."

Ronan grew up as a Cubs fan. His grandfather would take him to Wrigley Field, another magical baseball place, filled with men drinking beer and smoking cigars. That, he assumed, was what adult life smelled like in the outside world: cigars and beer. Baseball meant a magical place with a magical smell.

When he went to Boston for medical school, he was ready to slide easily from the always-troubled Cubs to the always-troubled Red Sox. When he stayed in town to prac-

tice at Massachusetts General Hospital, his adopted team
became his team. He was hooked.

"I had some patients from Louisville up here the day after
the Aaron Boone homer," Ronan says. "I took them out to
dinner at Antonio's. Being from Louisville, they don't know
much about all this. The man said—we're sitting at the
table—'What's the big deal? Everybody seems so upset.'

"The waiter was at our table. He heard the man. The
waiter grabbed his arm. Grabbed it very hard. Both hands.
'Twenty years ago, my father had a stroke,' the waiter said.
"He didn't talk for eighteen years. Then he spoke. I was
with him. The first words out of his mouth in eighteen
years were, 'How are the Red Sox doing?' I told him, 'Not
this year, Pop.' Two months later he died. What's the big
deal? What's the big deal? That's the big deal."

Ronan's tale from the Aaron Boone game was as good
as anyone's tale. He had to work late at the hospital, didn't
get out until the fifth inning, and worried that he wouldn't
get home in time to see the end of the game. He went to
one of the nearest bars he could find, which turned out to
be Grafton Street, a trendy singles kind of place in Harvard Square. The place was filled with young yuppie girls
looking for a date.

A middle-aged guy, Ronan went to the end of the bar to
study the baseball by himself. No one bothered him. In the
seventh inning, he heard one of the young yuppie girls say
to a friend, "Look at that pitcher. He looks really tired.
They should take him out." The pitcher was Pedro Martinez. Ronan had the same opinion. When Martinez came
out to pitch the eighth, the girl said again, "That guy looks

really tired. Why don't they take him out?" Ronan agreed again. Manager Grady Little did not agree.

"Here's this girl *who knows nothing about baseball,* and she can see Pedro's tired, *even though she didn't know his name,*" Ronan says, still agitated by the moment. "She knows and Grady Little doesn't know?"

He watched the end of the St. Louis game, the clincher, again by himself, this time at home. Midway through the game he turned off the television and took a radio and a bottle of champagne onto the porch. The smell of beer and cigars floated all the way from Chicago.

This was it. He says he felt a peace, felt better than he ever thought he would.

❖

Ehsan Farkhondeh (student):

"I'm from the generation that 2003 was our chance to join in the Red Sox pain," Ehsan Farkhondeh says. "I watched that Aaron Boone game at the fraternity house. There were maybe twenty brothers watching it on our sixty-three-inch television. When Aaron Boone hit that home run, there was no noise. Everything went dead. Even the Yankees fans didn't say a word.

"I just left. I had to move my car, so I got in, drove around for a while with my thoughts, then parked the car in Cambridge. I remember walking across the Harvard Bridge, cold, the wind blowing. The whole city just went quiet. You could feel it."

Farkhondeh, 22, is a senior at the Massachusetts Institute of Technology. Born in Boston, the son of Iranian parents, he picked up the Red Sox early and took them with him when the family moved to Hampstead, New Hampshire. He is a brother at Phi Sigma Kappa fraternity, whose house is on Commonwealth Avenue, close to Kenmore Square. It is the closest frat house to Fenway Park.

"We used to be able to see the Green Monster from the house, but they built the Commonwealth Hotel across the street," he says. "We can still see the lights, and when big things happen in a game you can hear the noise. It's nice. You can watch the game on television, then go outside when it ends and be part of the crowd."

His roommate Jerry Adler is from New York and is a Yankees fan. They talk baseball a lot. Jerry Adler always has had the last word, of course, in arguments. The roommates don't go to baseball a lot, didn't see a game in person all year because tickets are scarce and money is scarce and time is scarce if you're going to MIT, but they did watch on television. Farkhondeh went over to Fenway just to watch the players drive out of the parking lot, to see what kinds of cars they drive.

Following the playoffs and the Series was hard on an MIT schedule. Farkhondeh surrendered the four, five, six hours a night to do it. When he had a late class and a test that conflicted with the final game against the Angels, he watched the game on Tivo. Putting his fingers in his ears so he couldn't hear frat brothers trying to tell him the result and the details, he stood up and cheered for Ortiz's extra-inning homer about six hours after it happened.

For the Yankees series, he decided that he would wear

Red Sox gear for each game. If a particular piece of apparel worked he would stick with it. If not, he would go to his closet and find something else. Midway through the 19–8 loss in the third game, third loss in a row, he decided his approach wasn't working.

"That game was awful," Farkhondeh says. "Bronson Arroyo threw sixty pitches, and I think the Yankees hit every one of them. That was the low point. My roommate was laughing at me. I went onto the Web—Sons of Sam Horn—looking for consolation."

He found a post that grabbed him. Someone had written: "There is that tiny synapse in my brain, firing away, telling me that this is all an elaborate set-up to an Apocalyptic rising from the dead." Farkhondeh printed it out, typed it on a message that he sent to 150 friends. He showed it to everyone he knew.

Changing strategy, he decided to abandon not only Red Sox gear but all personal grooming for as long as the team could survive. Twelve days, eight wins, and one World Championship later, he was as unshaven and almost as long-haired as Johnny Damon as he ran out the door to join in the Kenmore Square celebration.

"A bunch of us went," he says. "We were out there after the Yankees series too. We didn't get into any trouble. I'd been around things like that before, and I knew that the police usually give people a little time to let off steam, then they start moving. We were gone, back in the house, watching it all on television by then."

There is a reason Ehsan Farkhondeh is at MIT.

❖

Esther Newberg (literary agent):

"I was in London when the Red Sox won the World Series," Esther Newberg says. "Don't ask. A long time ago, before you could see anything like this happening, Carl
Hiassen asked me to go with him to London. He doesn't
like to fly. He's all right flying over land, but he doesn't like
flying over oceans. His wife couldn't go and he asked me.

"So I went to London, and I watched every game from
like one until five in the morning. People say, 'That must
have been terrible, you must be exhausted.' Are you kid-
ding? This was the best thing ever."

The story could have come from one of Hiassen's comic
novels. Here was Newberg, a very public face for Red Sox
fandom in New York, New York, teased often by no less
than Don Imus on WFAN for her beliefs, Lobster Newberg forced into exile for the big moment. She had a list of
Yankees fans that could have run down Broadway it was so
long, people who had to be contacted when and if ever the
Red Sox won the whole thing. She was in London.

"I grew up with two idols," she says. "Ted Williams and
Frank Sinatra. I'm not sure why. There was something
about Ted Williams I liked.

"I grew up a Red Sox fan in Middletown, Connecticut.
My father was a Red Sox fan. We got the *Hartford Courant*
every morning at the house. The *Courant* spent more time
on the Red Sox than the New York teams. Rooting for the
Red Sox was easy."

She forgave her only sister for marrying a Yankees fan

(and a Republican) when her sister told her that she and her husband watched baseball in separate rooms, something they now have done for 46 years. The fact that seven of her sister's grandchildren are now Red Sox fans, not Yankees fans, is seen as evidence of strength on the Newberg side of the gene pool.

A couple of traumatic things have happened to Newberg while wearing her Red Sox hat to Yankee Stadium—a friend was punched in the side at the '86 Series, and a teenage boy spit at Newberg herself, full in the face, at the 2003 ALCS—and she will not go back. The most traumatic moment at a Red Sox–Yankees game, though, happened at Shea Stadium in 1975, the year when Yankee Stadium was being renovated. Newberg wasn't even there. Her father suffered a fatal heart attack.

"I was going out with this schmuck at the time," Newberg says. "I was in the process of breaking up with the guy, but it hadn't happened yet. My father has this heart attack at Shea—he was there with a bunch of his friends, most of them Yankees fans—and they take him to a hospital in Queens.

"It looked for a while like he was going to be fine, so the rest of the family had gone home. I was there with this schmuck. My father is lying in the bed, can't talk, so he writes on this pad, 'How did the Red Sox do?' The schmuck says, 'They won!' My father looks at me, and writes, 'I love you,' and then he dies. That's the last moment of his life."

A few weeks later Newberg and her mother were going through the bills, sorting out finances. They came across a $150 Visa charge her father had made on the night he died.

What was that? They thought a while, and Newberg decided that her father had bought dinner for his group of friends, the free-loading Yankee fans. She called one of them to make sure that was what happened, and he said it did. On a hunch, she asked a question that had been nagging at her since the final scene with her dad.

"Did the Red Sox win the game that night?" she asked.

"Oh no," the friend said. "They were losing big when your father became sick, and that was the way the game finished."

"That schmuck," Newberg said. "He lied."

The romance was officially done.

"I called my ninety-one-year-old mother after the win in St. Louis and asked her if she believed it," Newberg says. "She said, 'It's your father's legacy.'"

David Molloy (retired):

"My story starts back in 1952, when I was a country boy of ten years and had a love to play ball," David Molloy of Lower Sackville, Nova Scotia, says. "The only problem for me was that baseball was basically nonexistent where I lived, and my only satisfaction was about a thousand throws a day against an old barn and a good fielding percentage against rebounds.

"Then someone gave me an old radio, and fooling around with it that evening I picked up WHDH in Boston . . . just in time for a Red Sox game with Curt Gowdy and Bob Murphy. An entire new world opened up for me that night . . . a Red Sox world that runs right to this day."

Nova Scotia and the Maritime Provinces always have been Red Sox country, attached first by the flickering voices of Gowdy and Murphy, now by satellite and cable television. Molloy, son of a Canadian air force truck driver, but living in farm country, found that his radio pretty much only worked for Red Sox games at night. Too many other stations interfered during the day.

Someone told him that what he needed was an antenna. He went looking for something useful in a dump and came across some old fence wire. Tying assorted pieces of wire together, he strung them out for 500 yards from a tree in his backyard to his radio in the house. The voices of Gowdy and Murphy sounded as if the broadcasters were in the same room. The 500-yard antenna did the trick.

"Now my new world was complete," Molloy says.

He eventually wound up at Fenway Park four or five times, traveling to Massachusetts to visit relatives, seeing the Red Sox through the years as he married and raised kids and worked for Sears as a sales manager. His latest visit before this year, he figures, was 1986.

In the past few years, retired from Sears after 37 years, he has been battling cancer. The treatments have been tough, and the prognosis has been tough, and the summer of 2004 was not a very good time. The Red Sox were a beacon.

"It's so true, you wait for that game," he says. "It's a goal for everything you're going through during the day."

His son, also named David, knew the situation, knew

that if his father ever would go to a playoff game, a World Series, this probably would have to be the year. He wrote to Red Sox management and described his father's condition and asked if there was a possibility that he might buy two tickets to a playoff game against the Yankees. The Red Sox sent the tickets, no charge, for game three.

"I flew to Toronto and met my son, who flew in from Calgary," David Molloy says. "Then we flew together to Boston, where we arrived late and had to hurry to the park to make it by the start of the game."

This was the 19–8 destruction of the Red Sox by the Yankees. Neither Molloy said it mattered. They were at the game, at the park. They had the memory. Midway through the game the father noticed a strange occurrence. He was looking at the retired numbers on the right-field stands and noticed that the number 8, to commemorate Carl Yastrzemski, was different from the rest. It was glowing. A different color, perhaps. Something. Molloy is color-blind and couldn't say what was different for sure.

"Do you see anything different about the number 8 out there?" he asked his son.

"Looks like all the other ones to me," the son replied.

Molloy has felt premonitions before in his life. He thought this was another one. He simply couldn't figure out what it meant. The number 8? What was the significance?

"Then the Red Sox won the next eight games in a row," he says. "That was the number 8 I saw. The 19–8 game shook up the sleeping giant. That was the message. Eight in a row."

Molloy is on a new experimental chemotherapy treatment and hopes for the best. He says he has a new goal: to see opening day in 2005, when the Red Sox receive their championship rings. The Yankees are the opponents, and "I just want to see their faces."

7. The Story of the Baseball Tavern

THE CHOICES FOR PREGAME AND POSTGAME BEVER-
AGES around Fenway Park vary from the bars and clubs of
Lansdowne Street, catering to a young demographic, to the
Baseball Tavern on Brookline Avenue. The Tavern is a
basic, no-nonsense, I'll-have-a-Bud drinking establish-
ment. On a normal night seven regulars who all know each
other's first names will sit and discuss the plot lines of the
repeat episode of *Hawaii 5-0* showing on the television
screen. On a baseball night there will be madness in the
place.

A picture of Roger Clemens in his Red Sox uniform still
hangs upside down, placed that way after he took the
Toronto Blue Jays' money and left. The framed Montreal
Canadiens road jersey of owner Jimmy Rooney's brother
Stevie is on another wall. An expansion when the next-
door liquor store moved has brought certain amenities—
the first ladies' room in Baseball Tavern history, for
example—but the character of the place pretty much re-
mains.

This is where the celebrating Red Sox came after they
clinched a playoff berth in 2003, Kevin Millar standing on

the bar and ordering drinks. The ushers, the concession workers, the cops of Fenway drink here after games. This is where fans came in bulk to watch the Yankees fall in New York and see the World Championship won in St. Louis. The idea presumably was that if the games weren't at Fenway, well, we could be close to Fenway.

❖

Jimmy Rooney (owner):

"My father bought the place in 1963," Jimmy Rooney says. "He didn't buy it because it was close to the park. He bought it because this was an industrial area. There were three manufacturing companies within a few blocks. The Sears headquarters was here. My father had bars in Dorchester and South Boston, and he thought this was a good investment. He figured when the three shifts let out at all these places, guys wanted to come for a drink.

"Now the area's completely changed. The manufacturing places all have moved. Sears has moved. But the baseball has gone crazy. It's funny, ten years ago everyone was advising me to sell the place. Now it's a gold mine."

The money all is in the beer, $3.50 per bottle on game days. Arms reach out from a crowd two and three deep, bottle caps fly in the hour, hour and a half before games. The scene is repeated after games, larger if the Red Sox win. The crowd is predominantly male, but the number of women has increased since the ladies' room renovation.

"It used to be interesting with the one bathroom," Rooney says. "There'd be a line of guys, and a woman would ask if she could cut the line . . . or maybe she would stay in there for a while, fixing her makeup. Interesting."

A contingent of New York police and firemen appear every year for a baseball weekend and bring a back-and-forth edge to the room. They have fun. The locals yell the "Yankees suck" thing, and the policemen and firemen yell the "1918" thing in return.

Rooney grew up around the bar, grew up around the Red Sox. He slips over to the ballpark for four or five innings for most games, then slips back. He is hooked into the saga.

"The Aaron Boone game last year was the worst," he says. "I was at a wedding in New Jersey. The groom was from here, the bride from there. I had to watch with all of these Yankees fans. The Yankees fans go crazy, and I have to listen to them. I call the bar to see what's happening. They tell me that people are tipping over the tables and are all upset."

Rooney went to the final two games of the World Series. His father had made the same trip to St. Louis in 1967 but couldn't find tickets and wound up with his buddies watching the game in a bar outside Busch Stadium. This time Budweiser was interested enough in the Tavern and its baseball business to set up tickets in St. Louis.

Rooney went with a friend. Rooney wore a Red Sox hat to both games to show his allegiance. His friend, forgetting that St. Louis is a bit warmer than Boston, wore his lined Red Sox bullpen jacket. He sweltered in the heat but wouldn't take it off. He wanted the logo on his body.

When the game was done, Rooney's cell phone started ringing. He was hearing from ushers, concessionaires at

Fenway. (He runs an annual party for the ushers.) No one could believe the finish. Ushers who had worked at Fenway for 50 years were crying on the phone. Rooney cried back at them. He said he didn't leave his seat for two hours, spellbound. He came home the next day. The parade was two days later and started in front of his place.

"A guy told me for the parade that there were seventy thousand people crammed into this little area of Boylston Street," Rooney says. "I went up on the roof with Joe Zimmer. He's a big man. I had to push him through the hatch to get onto the roof. People were everywhere. It was an unbelievable sight—the parade, not pushing Joe Zimmer through the hatch."

The parade was being televised by NESN, the Red Sox station. Rooney and Zimmer were on the roof. Jason Varitek pointed up at them and waved. The camera panned up to Rooney and Zimmer.

"Look at those guys," announcer Tom Caron said. "They probably are in the calmest place in the Baseball Tavern. The doors opened, I think, at eight A.M."

The place was filled by eight-thirty.

Billy Donovan (teacher, bartender):

"I was working the bar in 2003 when the Red Sox clinched the wild card," Billy Donovan says. "The place was packed, and all of a sudden people backed away from the bar. I couldn't figure out what was happening. Then Kevin Millar and Todd Walker are right in front of me, still in their baseball uniforms, and Millar says, 'We're coming over the bar,' and I said, 'Okay.'

"Millar grabbed one of those big half-gallon Seagram's bottles with the jug handle and started nipping. Then Derek Lowe comes over the bar. He's a big boy. Then Gabe Kapler and Lou Merloni. They're handing out beers to people, drinking shots. It was crazy in there anyway, but for the ten, fifteen minutes these guys were there it was wild.

"They were leaving right from the park to go play at Tampa Bay the next day, so everything was in a hurry. On the way out Jimmy stopped Millar and asked if there was beer on the plane. Millar said he didn't think so. Jimmy told him to stop the bus at the door. We loaded on six cases of beer. That must have been a good plane flight to Tampa. Those guys must have been in good shape the next day . . . and I think they won."

Donovan, 23, is a sports hound. He can talk old-time with the old-timers, today with the kids. He is proud of the fact that both Dave Stewart and Fernando Valenzuela pitched no-hitters on his 13th birthday, June 29, 1994. He remembers that his uncle died on the day Carl Everett head-butted the home plate umpire Ron Kulpa. That is part of being a sports hound, tagging every memorable moment in life with a sports page headline. Donovan also is proud of the fact that Ron Kulpa has come into the Tavern and described the Carl Everett experience.

Donovan's cousin, Joe Zimmer, is another bartender. Joe Zimmer is the one who brought him to the altar of sport.

"I'm seven years old," Billy Donovan says. "I go to Fenway with my father, my brother, and Zimmer. Roger

Clemens is pitching a one-hitter. My father looks around in about the fifth inning. He says, 'Where's Billy?' Zimmer says, 'I don't know, but I did offer him five dollars if he'd climb the fence and walk to the mound and shake Roger Clemens's hand.' My father caught me just as I was about to climb the fence. I would have done it. Seven years old. Five bucks sounded like all the money in the world."

Zimmer worked a sausage cart underneath the bleachers when Donovan was young. Donovan would tag along. It was easy to get seats before every game was a sellout and sit in the first row of the bleachers. He would talk during games with Red Sox reliever Tony Fossas. The subject often would be why Fossas's curveball wasn't curving.

"He was very nice," Donovan says. "I think he was happy just to have someone talking to him, not booing him."

Working the Baseball Tavern's front door during the season, Donovan would take informal polls on Red Sox questions. Which free agents should the Red Sox keep and which ones should they not pursue? He would start debates in the line waiting to get inside the door. Pedro or Varitek? What about Lowe? Cabrera? The job didn't seem like a job. Get paid? For talking baseball?

"I like to talk with the guys who come down from Maine or from western Mass, places like North Adams," he says. "They want to talk some baseball. They're down here one time a year, right outside Fenway Park, and they want to talk about the game. I put myself in their place. That's exactly what I'd want to do—talk to someone who's around Fenway all the time.

"The average guy who comes in here, blue-collar, knows

that Billy Trauber, who the Sox just signed, was a first-round draft choice once. Could be a steal. He knows that when Mike Greenwell and Ellis Burks collided in the eighties, Greenwell kneed Ellis in the nuts. The other bars around here . . . Lansdowne Street, that's where my girl-friend goes with her friends. My girlfriend and them go to the game, wear the Manny T-shirts, but they also have the Gucci bags and the $150 shoes.

"Here, it's baseball. It doesn't matter what you wear."

Mark Linehan (bartender, radio personality):

"I worked the two important Wednesday nights in a row," Mark Linehan says. "It was amazing. I work one night a week at the bar, Wednesday, and the Red Sox beat the Yankees on one Wednesday in the seventh game, and then the next Wednesday they won the World Series in St. Louis.

"The place was packed both nights, but the reactions were entirely different. When the Red Sox beat the Yankees, everybody just went nuts and ran out of the place, into the streets. We were empty in like a minute. That was when there was all the trouble. The riot police. The whole thing. When the Red Sox beat the Cardinals, it was noisy, but just happy. Everybody was talking on their cell phones. You looked around the bar, and that's all you saw, cell phones. Everyone was calling someone, wanting to share the moment.

"The first night it was like looking through a plate-glass

window into downtown Fallujah. The second night it was just like New Year's Eve. The one thing that was the same . . . both nights people sprayed so much beer around celebrating that the lights went out. Something got wet, I guess. The lights went out for a minute. The cash registers locked up. It was something."

Linehan, 41, also works in the ticket office at Symphony Hall and as a radio voice around the country, appearing as different characters. He spouts Red Sox statistics on a rock show in Dublin in the voice of an Irish priest, listeners presumably wondering who Pokey Reese and this Manny Ramirez fella might be. One of the characters is Speedo the Brief, the World's Fastest Psychic. ("I say I was hit by a bus when I was twelve years old, and ever since then I have this strange power. People always nod. Not one of them ever— ever—has said, 'Gee, did you really get hurt?'") Speedo the Brief made a good prediction in 2003.

"The only thing that worries me about Wakefield is that he gives up home runs," he told Russell Hodsdon, ticket manager at Symphony Hall. They were sitting in a restaurant called Tiger Lily as the bottom of the eleventh inning began in the seventh game at Yankee Stadium.

"Like that?" Hodsdon said as the ball went into the left-field seats.

Linehan also has roamed the nooks and underbellies of Fenway for a lifetime. When he was five years old, he was at the 1967 World Series, brought by his brother. He was selling popcorn in the park on the day before the Bucky Dent game in '78. He figured out in the fourth or fifth inning, Red Sox ahead, that there was going to be a playoff the next day and headed straight to the ticket booth with his $80 in concessions money. The $80 was soon doubled as lines formed and people would pay bigger prices for those same tickets. He was on the other end at Shea Stadium in '86 with a girlfriend, buying tickets from a scalper in the parking lot.

The Red Sox have been a part of his everyday conversation for as long as he can remember. Figure out the strategies. Laugh about the failures. Try to figure out what comes next.

"I learned a great thing this year," Linehan says. "We were giving my eighty-five-year-old mother some grief, asking her about watching the 1918 World Series. She kept saying she hadn't even been born then. I looked it up, figured it out. She was born exactly nine months after the Red Sox won the Series. The way I figure it, Granny must have gone out for a night of celebration. One thing led to another. I'm Babe Ruth's grandson."

Linehan and Billy Donovan shut down the bar for the final half-inning of this clincher. They stood on the side and watched the final out of the final inning. Linehan called his mother. Everybody called someone.

"Think about this, remember this," Linehan told Donovan as the game ended. "This is something, twenty-five years from now, you'll remember where you were, what you were doing, who you were with. You'll tell people you were with me."

"Don't spoil the moment," Donovan said.

❖

Byron Burgess (bartender):

"I grew up in Alexandria, Louisiana," Byron Burgess says. "I was a little kid, and I had an uncle who went away to the Boston Conservatory of Music, then switched to the New England Conservatory of Music, and that's how I became a Red Sox fan. Thank God my uncle didn't go to the New York Conservatory of Music.

"I just loved the Red Sox. The Celtics too. When it came time for me to go to college, I went to Emerson College in Boston. A lot of the reason, I have to admit, is because that was where the Red Sox were."

Burgess is a bartender at the Crossroads, which is located maybe eight blocks from the Baseball Tavern on Beacon Street near Massachusetts Avenue, the other side of Fenway Park. He has been there for 13 years. This is an Irish place—owner Mike Broddigan's picture with Sien Fein leaders Gerry Adams and Martin McGuinness is displayed prominently behind the bar—but most of the clientele is college kids and, on game days, Red Sox fans.

"You'll see the same people every year," Burgess says. "You won't see them from the end of the season until opening day, but they'll be back. Season ticket holders. They'll have a bunch of beers after a win, one and done after a loss."

Burgess is part of the attraction. He is animated in all discussions about the team and its fate. He knows his baseball. He shouts during games. He cheers. He bleeds. He has his suffering stories:

"Game six, 1986, I watched the game at someone's apartment," he says. "The place was half Mets fans, half Red Sox fans. We lose the game, I don't say anything, take my girl-friend and leave. We're on the elevator, and this Yankees fan gets on. He says, 'You know, Byron, the Red Sox didn't give that game away. The Mets just took it away.' I started to swing at him, but my girlfriend and some other people grabbed me. The elevator stopped and the guy just ran off, fast as he could."

For game seven of 1986 Burgess was in a bar with his girlfriend. The game ended, Red Sox finished, and he turned and hit his head as hard as he could on a brick wall. Management brought some ice.

In 2003, seventh game, he drank in the Crossroads on his night off. The place was packed, maybe 200 people. Aaron Boone hit the home run, and people began leaving in a hurry. Ten minutes after the game, five people were left. Burgess still was steaming. The citywide smoking ban had been put into effect a few weeks earlier. He didn't care. He performed the biggest act of defiance possible in this new and safe 21st century: he lit up a Marlboro Light.

The bartender on duty cared. He told Burgess he was shut off for the night.

"Cut off at my own bar!" Burgess says. "And I wasn't even drunk. I wasn't."

He was working for the final game of the 2004 Series. He'd tried to handicap the games, figured that St. Louis had to win at least one, and had taken the next night off to watch the celebration. Now the celebration was one night early.

"I shut the bar down for the final out." Byron Burgess says. "I'd been waiting 29 years for this, and I wasn't going to be serving some guy a beer when it happened. I cheered and then went around the bar and started hugging people."

It seemed like the bar room thing to do.

8. The Victory Story

THE FINAL DIP ON THE 86-YEAR ROLLER-COASTER ride, the big one, obviously brought the most pleasure. The comeback against the Yankees was the grand excitement, with the finish against the Cardinals the smooth glide to the end where everybody, still dizzy, could stumble out of the car, dazed and exhilarated.

The general feeling was "whew." Everybody felt that, everybody who watched the games anywhere, but for some people the win had extra meaning. They were at the games. They were part of the noise, the howl. They had front-row seats for this particular amusement park ride, and so they held their arms up the whole way and screamed as loud as they could.

❖

Kate Reilly (new celebrity):

"I started putting stickers on my car in 1986," Kate Reilly says. "It started by accident. I saw a girl struck by a truck. It really bothered me. I put on some stickers, joined a group, SLOW PLEASE. Then I found other stickers. And people would give them to me. Nothing too controversial.

QUESTION AUTHORITY. Environmental stuff. No NRA. Nothing pro-life. The raciest one I had, I guess, was I REMEMBER WHEN ROCK CLIMBING WAS DANGEROUS AND SEX WAS SAFE.

"I had that car for sixteen years. My Jeep Grand Wagoneer. The car was totally covered with stickers except for the windows. It was kind of a spirit for the town. People always enjoyed it. It finally died, caught fire in Harvard Square. The town had a memorial service and everything. A wake. It was amazing."

Reilly bought her new car, the Pathfinder, in 2002. She vowed to her husband that her bumper sticker days were done. Then she fell in love with the Red Sox, and the Red Sox did what they did. Things happen.

She had liked the Red Sox since she was a girl, nice memories of listening to ball games with her uncle in Onset on Cape Cod. She and her sister would sit on his lap, three and four years old, and he would smoke his pipe and rock in his rocking chair and the baseball games from Boston would be on the radio. She didn't remember so much about the games and the names as she grew up, but remembered the feeling.

Her intense interest began maybe a decade ago and grew and grew. Her husband, a stockbroker from Marblehead, had owned season tickets for a long time, mostly for business reasons. Now the tickets started to be used for personal reasons as Kate fell further and further in love with the team, the games, the quest, the whole package. Her daughter Colleen took a job with the team two years ago as a Red Sox Ambassador, a feature of the new management, a liaison with fans. This brought the interest up another level for Kate.

"I put on warpaint for one of the Yankees games in 2003 in the middle of the season," she says. "I just took my lipstick—Crimson Flip or something like that by Revlon—and drew some lines under my eyes. Just for fun. I was with my oldest son, and he liked it. He hugged me and said, 'Mom, you're the best.' I started doing it for every game. The times I didn't do it, people would say, 'You're not going to do your face?' I'd go in the ladies' room and take out my lipstick.

"It's all about making the most of the moment. I'm fifty-eight years old and who cares? Make the most of the moment."

She tried face paint but, curiously, found it harder to remove than the lipstick. She stuck with Crimson Flip and would come home, wash with a soft towel, and think she had erased everything. Her husband would spot her pillow in the morning, totally red, and say, "Are you all right? It looks like you bled to death."

Kate's daughter Colleen began working on the field in 2004, running around the diamond in a hurry, sweeping off each base in the middle of the fifth inning, and that made the games even more of a hoot. As the season progressed and the playoffs arrived, every pitch seemed important. Kate Reilly painted her face for every game. She also wore a straw hat she had enhanced with a Sox giveaway scarf that had the word BELIEVE. She fastened it with duct tape. Some guys behind her seat one night kept yelling, "Believe in what? Duct tape?" It was funny.

The win over the Yankees, she thought, was great, and the World Series win was greater, but the parade was wonderful. The Fox cameras had found her in the postseason, showing close-up after close-up of this middle-aged woman with war paint, and when she went to the parade with her red face and straw hat, people recognized her.

She met a Russian man who was crying with joy. She met a man from Buffalo with two sons who had always promised them they would go to the parade if the Red Sox ever won everything. There they were. She met people from Arizona, Japan, Billerica, different places. Everyone was smiling.

"I just breathed a breath of spring and hope," Reilly says. "That was the feeling. It was wonderful. It didn't matter who you were or what you were, we were all the same. It was a wonderful experience."

In the morning the Boston newspapers were filled with pictures from the parade and from the season. Kate knew what she had to do. What else? She went to the hardware store, bought about 20 rolls of three-inch clear tape, and started taping the pictures and stories to her car, the 2002 Pathfinder. Her husband mentioned to her that she had promised that she would never tape over her car again. She told him, "Well, I lied."

So that is now her car. She stops for traffic lights and people can read about game seven against the Yanks, game four against the Cards, or maybe Curt Schilling's life story. Her idea is that the Red Sox's win and the parade felt so good that she wants to feel that every day when she gets in her car. Her car has become the parade.

A few days after the Series, car parked outside a gift shop in Beverly, she bought some World Series and Red Sox magnets. Souvenirs. The saleswoman tried to sell her some Red Sox World Championship flags for the car. Reilly looked and decided she didn't like them.

"I think they're a little ostentatious," she said.

The saleswoman couldn't stop laughing.

Ticket Man (ticket broker, name withheld):

"The World Series and the Yankees series were the biggest ticket ever," Ticket Man says. "I was *buying* tickets from people for $3,500 and *selling* them for $5,500. It was all just crazy. The walk-in price for bleacher seats on the street was $1,000. That's the first time that ever happened.

"The biggest ticket before this was the Patriots last year at the Super Bowl, where was it, Houston? I'll tell you how that happened. Three years ago the Patriots went to the Super Bowl in New Orleans. There were tickets everywhere. People went to the game at face value. They figured they'd do that in Houston too. I'll bet ten thousand people showed up without tickets.

"The World Series, though, was even crazier. I knew it was going to be good, but it was five times better than I thought. The corporations are the ones who pay $5,500 for a ticket. I guess it's good business for them. If someone's giving them $2 million in business, a couple of $5,500 tickets are worth it."

Ticket Man is a Boston guy. He grew up in a Boston

project. He scalped his first ticket outside Boston Garden when he was nine years old. He learned the back doors at Fenway, at the Garden, would sneak into a Boston Celtics game in the afternoon, find a dark, forgotten closet somewhere in the old building, sit inside with seven or eight friends, nobody talking for three hours until the gates were open again and they could go out and meld into the crowd and watch the Boston Bruins hockey game at night.

Moving tickets has been his business for his adult life. If tickets are involved and hard to find, he is involved.

"I used to get a bus, pick up homeless guys to stand in line for tickets to Jimmy Buffett," he says. "I had 208 guys in line one time outside the Orpheum Theater. That's where the Buffett tickets would go on sale. The homeless guys would buy the four tickets they were able to buy, then I'd send them back into line again. Some guys went through four times."

Ticket Man is a fan. He can still recite the "Impossible Dream" song and the Carl Yastrzemski song, but doesn't know the names of the streets in his present neighborhood. He does remember the names of all the bit players during the 1967 drive, remembers a game with the "Red Sox down, 8–0, and they come back against the California Angels. The Angels put in Paul Schaal for defensive purposes. Bases loaded, the ball goes through his legs, Red Sox win." Ticket Man had the heebie-jeebies when the Red Sox finally won it all this time. He was watching the final game of the Yankee series in his living room with his sons.

"It's 8–1," one son said. "It's the seventh inning. It's over."

"It's not over."

"It's 8–1."

"They're never going to win. You're too young. You don't understand."

"It's over, Dad. They won."

"I don't believe it."

Ticket Man says some counterfeit tickets were around for the World Series, very good replicas, a crew from New York, but they bounced at the gate because the holograms didn't work with the ticket scanners. Ticket Man also says that those late tickets the Red Sox put up for sale on the Internet, the "small number of seats available to fans," most of them went to brokers, who had crews with piles of credit cards working dozens of computers, a big operation in Phoenix. Ticket Man says June, July, and August always will be good at Fenway Park because it has become this baseball shrine and people come from out of town and want to get in the door. Ticket Man says he will be glad to help.

"What'll it be next year?" he asks. "Madness. Do you know the Red Sox are playing three games at Wrigley Field next year against the Cubs? What do you think those tickets will be worth?"

Jeff Horrigan (sportswriter, *Boston Herald*):

"One of my earliest memories is the Red Sox in 1967," Jeff Horrigan says. "I was three years old. I had brothers. We all learned the words to 'The Impossible Dream.' We ate Big Yaz bread. We knew the Yaz song too. Carl Yastrem-ski. Jess Cain at WHDH did it.

"In 1975, eleven years old, I watched the sixth game, the Fisk game, with my mother. She was sick with cancer and basically had been brought home to die. I was allowed to stay up late with her to see the game. She was a big Red Sox fan. This was her last shot to see the Red Sox win it and she knew it.

"You know how the chemo makes people's hair fall out? That was happening to her. While she was watching the game, she literally was pulling her hair out. I can see it. The game went into extra innings, and she was pulling out big clumps of hair."

Growing up in Dedham, Massachusetts, Horrigan papered his bedroom walls with Red Sox pictures from the newspapers. He cut out cartoons by Eddie Germano and Jim Dobbins of individual Sox players that ran in the Sunday comics. These too went on the wall.

He found a course toward future employment on a visit to an aunt's house. She had a plaque on her wall that the Red Sox had awarded his grandfather. Horrigan's mother, before she passed, had told him nothing about his grandfather. The plaque was inscribed to Jim Walsh, "in commemoration of your coverage of the Boston Red Sox." How about that? His grandfather was a sportswriter for the old *Boston Record*.

"I learned more about him," Horrigan says. "He was covering the team in 1918 when the Red Sox last won the thing. My aunt had a letter from him telling how the paper was sending down a certain society columnist to spring training, and the Babe and the other players were all worried about what she would write. It was very cool."

By the time the 1986 World Series rolled around, Horrigan had followed his grandfather onto the beat. After five years at Northeastern, stints at both the Associated Press and the *Globe* as an intern, he was at Shea Stadium for game six as the man from the *Manchester* (New Hampshire) *Union-Leader.* This was both a good thing and a bad thing.

The bad thing was that Major League Baseball tends to place writers from suburban newspapers in weird parts of the ballpark. The weirdness here was under a tent in the left-field stands, surrounded by Mets fans. Abuse came from all sides and in all forms. Mets fans said things, threw things, and one kept whacking Horrigan in the side. That was the major memory of the '86 Series. Abuse.

"Dave Henderson hit that home run early in game six, and it looked like the Red Sox were going to win the whole thing," Horrigan says. "There was a kid from the *New Bedford Standard-Times* sitting next to me. I forget his name, but he looked like either Seals or Croft, one of those singers, I'm not sure which one. He started jumping around and wanted to give me a high-five. I said, 'What, are you crazy? They'll kill us out here.' And they would have."

From Manchester he went to Cincinnati to cover the Reds, and from Cincinnati he returned home to cover the Red Sox for the *Herald.* He was plugged into the modern versions of those cartoon pictures on his boyhood wall. He was finding out the same things with the modern ballplayer that his grandfather found with the Babe.

"I did one of those twenty-question-and-answer things with Pedro Martinez in 2001, back when he wasn't so sour about everything," Horrigan says. "It was for *Sports Illustrated for Kids*. You know, what's your favorite color? What's your favorite food?"

The interview went like this:

Q: Favorite color?

A: Green.

Q: Favorite food?

A: Whatever.

Q: Favorite car? Favorite television show? Favorite book?

A: Whatever. Whatever. Whatever.

Q: Favorite actress?

A: Sandra Bullock.

Q: Secret ambition?

A: I would like to fuck Sandra Bullock.

Horrigan was not expecting this answer. He explained again that the interview was for *Sports Illustrated for Kids*. This answer about fucking Sandra Bullock probably would not go down very well with *Sports Illustrated for Kids*. Okay? Pedro nodded.

Q: Secret ambition?

A: I would like to sleep with Sandra Bullock.

Horrigan said maybe Pedro should answer that his secret ambition was to be a doctor. Pedro nodded.

Q: Secret ambition?

A: I would like to be a doctor.

"A big change happened with the Red Sox when the new management came in," Horrigan says. "The locker room became a lot more friendly. That's the way it was in Cincinnati, friendly, but I never thought it would happen here. You always knew, until these guys came in, that you were definitely the enemy in a Red Sox locker room.

"The Red Sox this year . . . I can honestly say that the best part of my day was going to the ballpark. The guys on this team didn't care about anything. I think that's how they did it, coming back from 3–0. Guys like Manny, David Ortiz, Johnny Damon, Bellhorn, you could explode a stick of dynamite in the middle of the locker room and they wouldn't notice. They would just keep doing whatever they were doing."

A force behind the new mood was Dr. Charles Steinberg, brought in from Baltimore by the new management as public relations director. Steinberg wore assorted hats. One of them was ad-hoc music director. He changed the music in the ballpark. He brought in "Sweet Caroline" in the eighth inning. He brought in "Dirty Water" after games. He found better candidates to sing the national anthem. He always was looking for musical additions. That was how the updated Red Sox song began.

Talking with Horrigan, a longtime and active rock music fan, Steinberg casually mentioned during spring training in 2004 that he thought it would be wonderful if some local band sometime recorded a modern rendition of "Tessie," the rallying song of the long-ago Red Sox Royal Rooters. He wondered why no one ever had done it. Horrigan immediately said he had a candidate.

"The Dropkick Murphys would be great at it," Horrigan said. "One of the things they do is take Irish traditional music and turn it into punk rock. This is perfect for them. And they love baseball."

Friends with lead singer Kenny Casey, he sent off an email detailing what the Red Sox wanted and needed. The band, named after an old-time drying-out facility for alcoholics in Acton, Massachusetts, was in Europe, but Casey immediately wired back: "I'm in." Horrigan found an old recording of "Tessie" and sent it in MP3 to Casey. The singer immediately wired back: "I'm out."

The song was tinny, dated, awful. The lyrics were about a woman telling her secrets to her parrot. The band heard the song and immediately called it "that fucking bird song." The one fact on its side was that it was written in B-flat, the only key that can be played by the bagpipes. Bagpipes were very big in the Dropkick Murphys. Casey, on second thought, asked Horrigan to write some new lyrics, bringing in baseball and old-time baseball names. Horrigan never had written song lyrics in his life.

"It turned out to be easy," Horrigan says. "I was really sick at the time. I had what turned out to be walking pneumonia. I was taking a bunch of antibiotics. I felt lousy, and I had to write this song, and someone suggested I try a beer. The beer and the antibiotics . . . I went to my room and wrote the whole song in about twenty minutes. I guess that's how you write a song, beer and antibiotics."

The Murphys updated the music. The lyrics fit fine. The whole thing worked. Seven months later the song was playing after the Red Sox had whipped the Yankees to stay alive to go back to New York, and the words were on the megaboard and people were singing along.

"Very cool," Jeff Horrigan says.

❖

Ken Casey (lead singer, Dropkick Murphys):

"The father of a friend of mine was a Boston cop," Ken Casey says. "In 1986 he got us into the final game of the Angels series in the ALCS. My friend and I, we were eighteen years old, the dynamic duo. The Red Sox won the game and the series, and we went down to run on the field and be crazy. Just when we were about to jump over the fence, my friend's father grabbed us. He took us to a souvenir stand, threw us inside, and locked us in.

"We were there for about two and a half hours. It was torture. The souvenir stand had a window onto the street. We could see all these kids, going crazy on the streets. That was exactly where we wanted to be except we couldn't get there."

A tattooed founder of a tattooed punk band, Casey doesn't look like the sports junkie that he is. He was raised in Milton by his grandfather, a Red Sox fan who was a union guy with enough connections to open Fenway back doors. He remembers running around right field in Fenway on an off day, pretending to be Dwight Evans. He remembers watching Freddie Lynn, his favorite player of all. Freddie Lynn and those diving catches. He remembers hours of watching baseball games at home with his grandfather.

How much time do you invest in baseball in a lifetime? Figure it out. Three hours per game, sometimes four. How many games per year? The time adds up. A chunk of your life is invested. The idea of singing a song for the Red Sox can become exciting.

"So Jeff sent the song to us in Europe, and it was just awful," Casey says. "I'm the one who had to present this idea to the band. It wasn't easy. The integrity and possibly the career of the band were at stake. But Jeff wrote the words, and I fooled around some with an acoustic guitar, and we decided to do it, and it turned out this was the perfect year to be involved with the Boston Red Sox."

The song was recorded in a studio next to the Baseball Tavern. Johnny Damon, Lennie DiNardo, Bronson Arroyo, Jeff Horrigan, and Dr. Charles Steinberg helped provide backup vocals.

The first time the Murphys appeared at Fenway to play the song was July 24. That was the game when Varitek punched A-Rod and Bill Mueller homered in the ninth and the return to pennant race respectability started. The Murphys seemed to be good luck. They became the unofficial Red Sox house band, the recorded "Tessie" part of the after-game show.

When the playoffs arrived, the Murphys played on the dugout at the pep rally. The team was in Anaheim, the fans were gathered at Fenway, and Casey looked down and saw that he was standing on top of the Red Sox logo. How great was that? People by now were singing along with Horrigan's words.

"You get new people at the ballpark," Casey says. "They know 'Dirty Water' and they know 'Sweet Caroline,' but they probably haven't listened to new music in twenty years. Even if ninety-nine percent of the people hate you, one percent of all Red Sox fans would be a pretty good group of people to bring in."

The band played live twice during the playoffs and the Series, both wins to finish with a 3–0 record in live appearances. Casey traveled to the games on the road. He was down by the dugout with a small knot of Red Sox fans in St. Louis when the Sox won the Series and the celebration began. He became part of the celebration.

"Charles Steinberg, my new favorite person in the world, got us onto the field," Casey says. "We didn't have credentials, so he said to just slide into the crowd and not be obvious. I got out there, though, and two minutes later I'm kneeling on the pitcher's mound, digging up dirt, and putting it in all my pockets. I look and there's my buddy, he's running around the field with Pedro Martinez, who's holding the trophy."

The friend was Tim Brady from Milton. He was the other half of the dynamic duo from 1986. No souvenir stand this time.

"I called my grandfather from the pitcher's mound," Casey says. "He was born in 1918, two days after the last World Series win. It was touching to hear him, how excited he was. I was excited too. I always had a thought that I would be on the field when the Red Sox won the World Series. I just expected some guy with a billy club would be chasing me."

David McCarty (baseball player):
"The days, the games, everything was just surreal," David McCarty says. "I was exhausted, going on very little

sleep, plus I was sick. I had a cold. A lot of guys on that team had colds. I'd come home, and it would be just hard to wind down. I was taking Nyquil for the cold, so that pretty much put me to sleep."

McCarty, 35, had perhaps the best seat available to watch everything that happened with the Red Sox in October of 2004. A combination outfielder–first baseman–pitcher during the season with the Red Sox with a .278 batting average, four home runs, and 17 RBI, he was caught in the numbers crunch for the postseason and left off the 25-man roster.

He still could dress in the uniform every night, still could sit in the dugout, just couldn't play. He was—one way to look at it—a professional fan. He was a big fan.

"I'd sit on the cooler in the dugout for every game," he says. "There are two coolers, the Gatorade and the water. It became very complicated on which cooler everyone sat. The coolers were about the one superstition we had in the dugout. If you sat on one of the coolers, you had to make good things happen."

McCarty, a Stanford graduate, took charge of the rotations. He would put himself on one of the coolers for the first three or four innings, but if nothing good was materializing, changes would be made. The various benchwarmers took turns trying to bring a proper karma to the scene. These mainly were the players like McCarty who were ineligible to play.

"We tried Mientkiewicz once," McCarty says about opening a cooler spot to players on the roster. "Didn't work."

McCarty, now with eleven years in the major leagues,

joined the Red Sox in the middle of the 2003 season, acquired off waivers from the Oakland Athletics. He had played with six different teams but never had played for a team on the East Coast. He wondered if he would like Boston.

"It's truly a different experience for a player," he says. "The people are so interested, so involved. I live in California, and I played for the A's, but I could spend a whole day doing errands without anyone recognizing me. Not in Boston. People not only knew who you were, they knew everything about you. I couldn't go a block from my house and someone would be asking me questions."

Part of the reason might have been that he lived with his wife and two kids only a few blocks from Fenway in an apartment at 75 Peterborough Street. A number of players—Kevin Youkilis, Pokey Reese, Orlando Cabrera, Mike Timlin, Lenny DiNardo, Curtis Leskanic, a bunch of them—lived in the same apartment house. They could walk to work.

McCarty liked the experience in Boston. He liked the fit, both in the town and on the team. He liked the excitement, 35,000 people sitting in the seats every day, waiting for the players to perform. He liked the team. Roles seemed to be handed out on merit, performance. He was happy enough with his seat on the bench.

"If I were twenty-five instead of thirty-five, it might be different," he says, "but this was fine. It was never the situation where you looked at a guy in front of you and you knew you were better than him and everyone else knew you were better than him and the guy still played because he was supposed to be 'a prospect.' There wasn't anything like that here. This was a team with talent."

The good seat on the bench led to a great champagne shower for McCarty in the locker room after game four in St. Louis and a great plane ride home. He received a full World Series share. He also had a good seat on one of the ducks for the parade through the city.

"It was just an incredible experience," he says. "The noise was deafening, louder than anything I've ever heard in any stadium. People would come up to me and say, 'Thank you,' and you could see they really meant it. I would say, 'Thank you,' in return."

❖

Leslie Epstein
(novelist, head of the Creative Writing Department, Boston University):
"I chose the Red Sox to root for primarily because they weren't the Yankees," Leslie Epstein says. "I grew up in California, and my team was the Hollywood Stars. There was no major league baseball in California at that time. My heroes were guys you never heard of. Mike Sandlock and Pinky Woods. Chuck Stevens. Jim Baxis. My all-time favorite, Frank Kelleher, just barely had a brush with the major leagues. These were the guys I watched at Gilmore Field.

"When I came east to go to college, all I knew was that I couldn't root for the Yankees. I was a Democrat, and they were against everything I stood for. They were big business, pinstriped suits. United Steel. I had eyes for the Red Sox. It was a curious choice because of their history, the racism and everything, but they had a literary quality. I don't know what it was. Writers liked them."

Epstein was a writer. His father, Julius, was one of the most well-known screenwriters in Hollywood. Julius, teaming with twin brother Phillip, had written *Casablanca*, *Arsenic and Old Lace*, *Yankee Doodle Dandy*, and scores of other movies and plays. The Epsteins knew a story with good plot lines. The Red Sox were a good choice.

For a while, Leslie Epstein's affection for the team was shown from a distance. He took a teaching job at Queens College in New York and remembers being in Vermont, trying to write a novel, when the 1967 excitement happened. He would take a transistor radio and walk around the woods trying to get better reception. In 1975 he remembers pulling over by the side of the road to listen to big moments of the World Series.

In 1978, just in time for the big late-season Red Sox fold and the Bucky Dent moment, he took a job at BU and moved his family to Brookline. One of the extra benefits of the move was that now he lived within walking distance of Fenway Park. His kids were young, twin sons and a daughter, and he would take them to nine or ten games per year.

He was surprised at how quickly his children took to the game. One of the twins was discussing strategies when he was eight years old. Sound strategies. Leslie Epstein soon thought that this kid, eight years old, maybe nine, knew as much about baseball as he did. Maybe more.

In 1986 the Red Sox drama was played out in different

venues for the Epsteins. Leslie took his sons to one of the games at Fenway. ("My son asked me just the other day how we got those seats. One of my students, Michael Giles, was the son of the owner of the Philadelphia Phillies. He got the tickets for us.") For game six, the family was at home, the boys standing on the couch in suspense, waiting for the celebration that never came. For game seven, the family was at neighbor Kana Kanerak's house for her 40th birthday party. Everyone was watching the television, and Kana, who was from South Africa and didn't appreciate baseball, went to the roof to see if she could unplug the antenna so the party could be a real party. She failed, alas, and everyone watched the grim end.

"Our favorite player was Jim Rice," Epstein says. "We were at that game when the foul ball struck the kid in the face. Everybody else froze. Nobody knew what to do. Jim Rice came out of the dugout and went into the stands and carried the kid to medical assistance. That was a man. He came out for the next inning and there was blood on his shirt."

Epstein's children are grown now, graduates of Yale and Wesleyan, and Epstein has found ways to go to a lot of baseball. He was in Yankee Stadium when Aaron Boone hit the home run, an experience so painful he vowed never to go back to the place. He went to the Yankees playoff games in Boston this year, skipped New York, then was in St. Louis for the two final games of the World Series. He was surprised at how fulfilled he felt at the end.

"I'm a glass half-empty guy, but my glass is filled over the top," he says. "I really wanted John Kerry to win the election—would have traded the Red Sox for it—but watching the Red Sox win was the greatest experience of my life outside of the births of my children."

His daughter, Anya, was in Los Angeles, finishing up a screenplay, but his wife and sons were with him in St. Louis. The married son, Paul, was with his wife. The unmarried son, the one who knew all of that baseball at eight years old, the one who came back to Boston to take a job three years ago, the one Leslie advised with only two words, "be bold," was working.

Theo Epstein, 30-year-old general manager of the Red Sox, had listened to his father. How about that? Boldness worked.

9. The Moral of the Story

THE BALLBUSTERS MET AT THE BARN BEHIND BABE Ruth's old house in Sudbury, Massachusetts, on the night of October 27, 2004. They had gathered there on October 25, 1986, when the ball skittered through Bill Buckner's legs on the red dirt of Shea Stadium and all of this curse business really started in earnest. It seemed fitting that they returned for the end.

"What are you doing this time?" one of the Ballbusters had asked Dennis Gavin in the morning, when the Red Sox were ahead, three games to none, and on the verge of capturing their first World Series in 86 years.

"Might as well do the same thing," Gavin said on impulse.

"I'll call the guys," the Ballbuster said.

It was as easy as that. On the night the Red Sox clinched with their 3–0 win in St. Louis, Gavin's old modified slow-pitch softball team from the Sudbury Park rec league toasted the moment in the spot where the Babe used to raise pit bulls and chickens. There were a dozen players, just about the same cast that had assembled 18 years earlier to watch the last World Series that was supposed to be won and wasn't. Their bodies told them how long the wait had been.

"It's that slow progression, isn't it?" Gavin, 53 years old, says. "The team was formed in 1983–84. You go from A league to B league, then to C league. You start out cheering the home runs and wind up cheering the solid singles to left. I finally gave it up last year. Nineteen years . . . but I still hang around with the guys. I'm still an honorary Ballbuster."

Gavin is the owner of Babe Ruth's old 15-room farmhouse, which he purchased 20 years ago as a fixer-upper. Part of the fixing was converting the barn—"which is huge," he says—into a recreation room. Neighbors say he has done a wonderful job. He had a party the night the Red Sox won game seven against the Yankees, plus the party for the clincher. He did his part to eliminate all potential curses.

"It's been great stuff," Gavin says. "Especially for my son. He loves baseball. He eats it, sleeps it, dreams it. He's loved every minute of this."

Notoriety had edged closer and closer to the house on Dutton Road since 1986, when the stories about the Curse of the Bambino began. The Babe lived there during his Red Sox career and for part of his time with the Yankees. The house was close enough to Fenway Park, maybe 30 miles, to be linked to the Red Sox's problems. Divers searched a nearby pond for the piano the Babe allegedly pushed through the ice one winter. Was that the start of the curse? Was he mad about being traded? Reporters arrived, asking questions about the house. Do you ever hear ghosts? It was all tongue-in-cheek fun.

Then the curse hit even closer. The date was August 31, 2004. Gavin has season tickets at Fenway, seats along the right-field foul line. He took his 16-year-old son, Lee, and his son's classmate, Jarrett Lowe, to the Angels game to celebrate Lowe's birthday. In the middle of the game, Manny Ramirez hit a ball that hooked right of the pole and struck Lee in the face, knocking out two teeth. Lee was hurt for the moment and minus the teeth, but soon was fine. He was better than fine. He was famous.

Lee Gavin became The Kid Who Broke the Curse.

The story started locally, then spread across the country. Maybe the Babe was looking for a blood offering and this was it! The kid in the Babe's house had surrendered two teeth! It didn't hurt the story that on the same night the Yankees were beaten 22–0 by the Cleveland Indians, the worst defeat in Yankees history. Reporters asked questions. The Kid Who Broke the Curse smiled, showed where the teeth had been.

The biggest moment came after the Series ended. Jay Leno called. Dennis and Lee flew to California, where Lee sat in the audience and Leno, a native of Andover, Massachusetts, came down and talked with him about the end of the curse during the monologue. Five Red Sox players also were on the late-night show—David Ortiz, Derek Lowe, Mike Timlin, Alan Embree, and Dave Roberts—and when the taping was finished, Dennis and Lee were invited backstage. Lee had brought a bag of baseballs with him. They were all signed.

The kid who lives in Babe Ruth's house was buzzing the way everyone buzzed. The Red Sox, the World Championship, the whole thing. Maybe he was buzzing even more. Headlines, cameras, Leno. He was 16 years old.

His father had one quiet message for him on the plane ride home.

"It's over now," Dennis Gavin said. "Get your feet back on the ground. It's time to settle down and get some grades."

A rough estimate is that 13,000 baseball games were played by Red Sox teams between World Championships. Some statistical wizard no doubt will go back and figure out the exact number, which probably will be higher, but 13,000 seems like a good estimate. (That's 150 games per season, times 86 years, for a total of 12,900. Throw in another 100 games for the heck of it.) Thirteen thousand seventh-inning stretches. Thirteen thousand national anthems. Twenty-six thousand trips to the men's room for the average patron if he went twice per game.

Some advertising wizard no doubt will figure out that if all the portions of a certain product that were consumed during Red Sox ball games—say, Cheetos, or hot dogs, or stalks of celery—were laid end to end, the distance would take a traveler from Boston to Mars or Jupiter or maybe Phoenix, Arizona. The *Boston Globe* already has pointed out that a loaf of bread was 10 cents when all of this began in 1918, eggs were 37 cents a dozen, a gallon of gas was a quarter, and the average cost of a home was $4,821. A flight between Chicago and New York took ten hours, five minutes.

Ted Williams was born on August 18, 1918, Dr. Billy Graham on November 7, Nelson Mandela on July 18. The streak of losing pretty much covered their lifetimes.

Eighty-six years is a very long time. A 95-year-old man from Winthrop, Massachusetts, was asked by a television reporter during all of the excitement in 2004 to comment on his memories of the 1918 World Series. "Christ," he said. "I was only nine years old." A long time.

The first important date in the story really was 1967. Everything before that, from the storied sale of Babe Ruth through the troubles of the Ted Williams teams in the late forties against the Yankees and the Cleveland Indians and the Cardinals was mere prelude. The Red Sox were simply another team in the chase behind the big-money business operation in the Bronx. The 1967 season, the Impossible Dream, was the turnaround, the rebirth of local interest.

In 1966 the attendance at Fenway Park was 811,172 for a team that finished in ninth place. This was the sixth consecutive season that attendance was under a million. Fenway, built in 1912, was already judged to be too old, too small, a liability. Baseball was not a great local interest.

The four-team pennant race and the Red Sox's survival at the end, capturing the pennant and heading off to face the Cardinals in the Series, brought 1,727,832 people to the park. Fenway wasn't old anymore; it was funky.

"What do you think of the ballpark?" a reporter asked Cardinals ace Bob Gibson in a famous exchange.

"Where's the second deck?" Gibson replied.

The children who fell in love with the Impossible Dream, the baby boomers, became the core of the future

Red Sox audience. They loved Yaz and Lonnie and Ken "The Hawk" Harrelson with his Nehru jackets and waterbed and gold chains. Tony Conigliaro was an important figure, walking off the ball fields of the North Shore, straight from St. Mary's High in Lynn to right field with the Red Sox. If he could do it, then couldn't any local kid do it? Tony C. was magic. The team was magic. The magic stayed with the boomers for the rest of their lives, and they handed it to their children. Five different people in this book began to sing the Yaz song while they were being interviewed.

"I had the call of the last out of the season, 'a pop fly, Petrocelli under it . . . he's got it,' on my answering machine until a couple of years ago," Geoff Hobson, who now lives in Cincinnati, says. "The kids finally made me take it off. Nobody knew what it meant. They were embarrassed when their friends called."

The boomers were the ones who tromped through the jungles of frustration in the seventies and into the eighties. They still can recite the details of Ed Armbrister's interference with Carlton Fisk in '75, the lack of a call by home-plate umpire Larry Barnett. ("We booed his brains out at Fenway whenever he showed up to do a game after that.") The blown lead and the Bucky Dent playoff loss in 1978. The good teams that were never good enough.

The Buckner Moment and 1986 were the true grand catalysts for the story of losing. The boomers now had 19 years on the Red Sox beat. They were married, and many had children who were old enough to understand and to cry. The saga took off when Dan Shaughnessy wrote *The Curse of the Bambino* in 1990 and gave the frustration a name and an identity. Some very good Oakland A's teams in the play-offs in 1988 and 1990 contributed. The Indians in 1995, the Yankees in 1999, and then again in 2003, completed the picture.

It was 37 years after the Impossible Dream when the 2004 ALCS and Series rolled around. The 20-year-old boomer of 1967 was now a definitely mortal 57-year-old. The 10-year-old of '67 was 47. Children of these people now had children. The legacy of losing, embellished by the numbers from before the Impossible Dream, witnessed by a growing population afterwards, had been stamped in the New England character and become part of everyday life.

To have it end in the way it did, a 12-day reversal of fortune that included disposing of the accursed Yankees, was drama of the highest order. It wore people out, wrung them out, kept them up into the middle of the night, sent them into their workdays with a new and different energy.

This wasn't a once-in-a-lifetime event. This covered a bunch of once-in-a-lifetimes, generations of once-in-a-lifetimes. Never will there be a sports moment in Boston, Massachusetts, that will bring so much joy to so many people. Never will there be such a release of emotion. Talk about delayed gratification.

Who didn't watch? Who didn't care?

The players will be remembered forever around New England, no matter what they do next in these free-agent times. They were the Dutch boys who finally put their fingers in the dike, the Jacks who climbed the impossible Beanstalk.

Sculptors will be here any day now to start whacking at hunks of marble to memorialize them all. The directions will be obvious. Make David Ortiz look powerful. Make Manny look unconscious. Use a little creativity to show the blood on Curt Schilling's ankle. Have fun with Johnny Damon's hair. With Pedro's hair. With everybody's hair. Show Kevin Millar talking, Jason Varitek standing tall, Orlando Cabrera turning the double play. Make a special statue, perhaps, memorializing Dave Roberts's steal of second base. Show the umpire signaling "safe."

Put out the books. Pump up the volume. Move the CDs, the DVDs, and the bobble-head dolls. Name a dish in the North End after the manager. (Would you like the Chicken Francona or the Lobster Mirabelli?) Take Theo Epstein on the talk-show circuit to tell people how to clean up, shape up, and be a success by the age of 30.

These were the people who answered the long-standing call. They were the firemen who coaxed the black cat off the roof where it had sat for 86 years. They beat the Yankees. They made dreams come true. This was the only ending that ever could have worked, a flag on top of a pole at Fenway Park. There had to be a sunset. There had to be a slow fade, strings in the background. This undeniably was it. This was the moment.

So what did it all mean? The attraction of sport is that it produces synthetic emotions. The winners feel happy and the losers feel sad, and everybody goes back to work in the morning. There is no blood lost in sport, at least for the spectators. Nobody dies. Nobody loses a house or a job or spouse or golden retriever. Sport is like books or movies or painting. It is a diversion. It doesn't have even the life-and-death struggle of gardening.

The Red Sox story, glorious as it was, was no different . . . and yet, it felt different. Didn't it? It felt more serious. It felt like there was more substance, heft, bone and gristle. Didn't it? This seemed to be more than a game, more than a bunch of games, more than a bunch of games over a bunch of years. This seemed to be a part of life.

What did it all mean? A fourth-grade teacher named Katrina Fujita asked her students that very question at the Solomon Schechter Day School of Greater Boston the day after the comeback was completed against the Yankees. This is what some of her kids wrote:

It makes me feel that anybody can do anything if they put their minds to it. It tells people to try their hardest even if they are not winning. It shows that you shouldn't be like, "I am so going to win," because you might not. It makes me think that miracles can happen. It tells you that there are no curses. It shows you to believe in yourself.
—Jordana Gardenswartz

I feel great that the Red Sox won. God helped them win. If he helped them, he can help me, too. God can help anyone.
—Kayla Wies

I feel that I can do anything, anything and I should never give up. I feel that I should always try my best and no matter what happens I should feel good because I tried.

—Madison Rodman

Never give up. Try your hardest. Keep the faith.

—Gavi Kaplan

You should never give up or you will never reach your goal. Always believe in beating someone you've never beaten.

—Jacob Fisher

I learned that if someone is creaming you and the game's not over you still can win. If a person used to be good and now they're bad it doesn't mean they stink and stay that way.

—Jacob Aaronson

I learned that you're down, but you're not out. You can't give up; you still have to try your hardest. If you're winning and you only need to win one more game, you still have to try your hardest.

—Alex Beshansky

It makes me feel like I'm stronger. It makes me feel like I can do anything. It makes me feel happier. It makes me feel like I can believe in anything.

—John Chartock

The win—the ending—meant whatever each particular person wanted it to mean. The fourth-graders probably went to the core—the idea that nothing is impossible, that hard work and faith will triumph in the end if you just keep going—but this was a personal story. Everybody attached his or her own meaning or importance to it depending on age and situation and time and passion involved. There is a middle-aged curmudgeon in Brookline, Massachusetts, who hated all of this. He thought it was silliness of the first order. Long before the players started calling themselves "idiots," he was using the word to describe everyone who lived and died with the fortunes on Yawkey Way. ("Don't put my name in this book," he says now. "I'll be arguing with idiots all day. I have to do business with some of them.") It wasn't that he didn't like baseball, he did, he simply didn't like the romanticizing of the great quest. Baseball was baseball. A game.

To handle the grand hoo-ha at the end, the middle-aged curmudgeon in Brookline put himself in what he called "a news blackout" for all of October 2004. He refused to watch the evening news, any news, for fear he would see all the bubbling faces at some bar, some street corner, a microphone stuck in front of them, everyone babbling about "the Sox." He pretty much refused to read.

"I'd open my front door every morning," he says. "I'd slide the folded *Globe* out of the plastic. I'd turn my head while I opened it up. I'd peek at the right-hand corner of the front page, because that's where they usually would run the score and some little sentence about the game. If the Red Sox won, I'd fold the paper back and throw it away. If they lost, I'd figure it was safe. I'd find out what was happening in the world."

Everyone had a story. Even the curmudgeons.

❖

The sports columnist in Hartford, Jeff Jacobs, asked readers to email in their stories about where they were and what they were thinking at the final moment. The responses were more of the wonderful same, stories of lost relatives and newborn babies and thanks and celebrations. The winner was from Jared Dolphin, a young prison guard from Middletown, Connecticut, who works at the Corrigan facility in Montville, Connecticut.

He grew up as a twin. His brother, Jason, was always a little bit bigger, a little bit faster, a little bit stronger. Jason was a Yankees fan. Jared chose the Red Sox. Their mother was from the Bronx, their father from upstate Connecticut. It all seemed to fit quite well.

Dolphin was working at the prison on the night the Red Sox beat the Yankees in the seventh game. He watched the end in the cell block. Moved by what he saw and felt, he wrote out his thoughts longhand during the night, then transcribed them and sent them to Jacobs. This is what Dolphin wrote:

> There it was—the last out. I don't mind admitting that I, a 30-year-old, 180-pound uniformed officer surrounded by a block full of thugs, wept like a baby. This was more than a game. This was every frustration I've

ever felt being washed away. This was payback for my tire that blew out the month before, the fight my girl and I had gotten into last week, that D+ I got on my report card back in eighth grade. This was a moment of reconciliation, payback for every God-awful thing that had happened in my life. . . .

Suddenly the block erupted. I bristled immediately and instinctively my hand reached for my flashlight. It was pandemonium: whistling, shouting, pounding on sinks, doors, bunks, anything the cons could find. This chaos was against every housing rule in the book, so I jumped up, ready to lay down the law. But as I stood there looking around the block I felt something else. I felt hope. Here I was, less than ten feet away from guys that will never see the outside of prison again, guys with problems worlds different from mine. The guy in the cell to my immediate left had 180 years, he wasn't going anywhere anytime soon. But as I watched him scream, holla, and pound on the door I realized he and I had something in common. That night hope and joy beamed itself into his dreary existence as well. As a Red-Sox fan we had watched the impossible happen, and if that dream could come true why couldn't others?

Instead of marching around the block trying to restore order I put my flashlight down and clapped. My applause joined the ruckus they were making and for five minutes it didn't stop. I applauded until my hands hurt. I was applauding the possibilities of the future. I was applauding dreams that I had left in limbo, dreams

that had seemed just as impossible as the Sox victory
that night. Maybe I would go back to college somehow
and maybe, just maybe, I could fulfill my dream of being
a writer. I'd find a way, just like Theo Epstein and his
Red-Sox had found a way to win tonight. In my mind
they had won it all, even before the World Series pres-
ents its own particular brand of worry. Let's face it, beating New York, the juggernaut, in a best-of-seven series
is far more of an accomplishment than beating St. Louis
or Houston, even if it happens to be in the World Series.
If Boston could win in the face of extreme adversity, why
couldn't I?

Thank you, Boston Red Sox. Thank you for giving
this young man a new hope for the future.

Officer J. Dolphin
CT Department Of Correction
Corrigan-Radgowsi CC

The stories are the story. They are oral history now. They
will get harder and harder to explain as new listeners come
along. ("People seriously believed there was a curse? People
went to cemeteries to visit their departed relatives when it
all was done? People wandered the streets, cried, hugged,
burst out of their skins? All this for a baseball game?" The
words are spoken in the past tense already.)

It will be like driving past the old high school, looking at
those brick walls and the windows and the playing fields
out back. Was I really there for four years? Everything
seemed so important. I agonized so much over so many
things. What was it all about? Time will convert passion

into memory, each year covering the experiences with another layer of the busy present.

And yet . . .

All of this was real. It all happened. The manufacturers of moments—television and print, packagers and salesmen—tried to take an enduring tale for their own, especially near the end, slap a "Curse of the Bambino" and "Red Sox Nation" brand on it all, and market it like toothpaste, but it was much deeper than that. This was family, gathered around the table, year after year, a perpetual Thanksgiving dinner. Everybody had a piece of it, everybody had a say, young and old, male and female, the richest of the rich and the poorest of the poor. Pass the potatoes and fire the manager. Give me the string beans and a closer who can get somebody out. Nothing like this will ever happen to us again, nothing that will bond us in exactly the same way, the connections between family and friends and flat-out strangers made solid by long fires of disappointment.

The stories are the story. They will never leave. Where were you for the final game in St. Louis? The seventh game of the Yankees series? Who was with you? Remember all of those other years, the sad finishes? Remember that time in the bleachers, the loudmouth who'd had too much beer? Remember Grandpa Jack, cigarette hanging out of his mouth, fixing the car and listening to the games? Remember?

There always will be time to talk. You will tell your story about the wondrous year of 2004, the year it all ended, about where you were and whom you were with and what you did and how you felt. I will tell you mine.

10. My Story (Coda)

I WAS CALLED BY THE PUBLIC RELATIONS DEPARTMENT of *Sports Illustrated* in April 2004 to appear on a panel to discuss sports in Boston. *SI* was celebrating its 50th anniversary, and part of the celebration was a traveling tent show of mementos, blown-up pictures of *SI* covers, and interactive games. The show was going to all 50 states in 50 weeks, each visit coinciding with lists of Best Athletes and Greatest Moments and articles about the particular state that would appear in the magazine that week.

The Boston visit came on the best local sports weekend of all, the annual Patriots Day weekend of the Boston Marathon. This one was even better than usual. Not only was the city filled with runners and their friends and families, but the New York Yankees also were in town. The weekend was a sports zoo, a menagerie.

This was the first visit of Alex Rodriguez as a Yankee. This was the first meeting with the accursed infidels of Steinbrenner since the letdown of the previous October when the Sox had lost the pennant. T-shirts questioning A-Rod's masculinity and the Yankees' dietary habits were everywhere. Conversations about the games abounded.

The *SI* operation was set up in a Boston University parking lot in Kenmore Square, directly across Commonwealth Avenue from the Pizzeria Uno. The start time on Saturday afternoon was five o'clock, perfect for spectators who had gone to the Yankees game at Fenway. The planning couldn't have worked better. On Friday night, exactly six months after surrendering the Aaron Boone homer, Tim Wakefield shut down the visitors, 6–2. On Saturday, game just completed, newcomer Curt Schilling beat them in a 5–2 win. Manny Ramirez homered. The invited guests—mostly advertisers and their friends—were in a buoyant mood.

The panelists on the stage were, left to right, Bob Cousy, Mike Eruzione, Doug Flutie, David Ortiz, and me. ("Holey-moley," the little kid shouted. "Shut up," I shushed.) *SI* does not fool around when it stages events. Not many groups could override this one—Cousy and the Celtics glories, Eruzione and the 1980 hockey miracle in the Olympics, Flutie and the Hail Mary pass for Boston College at Miami, and Ortiz, already the designated Red Sox teddy bear—as representative of Boston sports glory. (New England Patriots quarterback Tom Brady, fresh from the Super Bowl, was scheduled to appear on the same stage on Sunday.)

SI writers Ed Swift and Tom Verducci also sat at the long table. Swift was at an end, the emcee, designated to ask everyone else questions. I sat between Verducci and David Ortiz. The crowd was at our feet, looking up at all of us.

"Tell me this," Verducci whispered. "Don't you have a

strong feeling that we're on the wrong side of this table? Shouldn't we be down there?"

"Uh-huh," I whispered back.

The hour was delightful. Swift asked good questions. People in the crowd asked even better ones, a microphone passed from hand to hand. The athletes answered with humor and charm. Verducci and I kept our answers to a minimum, trying to stay as unobtrusive as possible.

I remember three things:

1. A woman in a New York Yankees jersey and hat asked Eruzione if he would appear at her daughter's birthday party on a certain date. Everybody laughed. He thought about his answer for a moment, then said, "I'll check my schedule. If I can do it, I promise I will do it. I mean that. I'll do it. You just have to do one thing for me. Take off that Yankees shirt and hat and burn them."

The crowd cheered. The "Yankees suck" chant was quite loud. The woman shook her head back and forth, wouldn't do it. The crowd became louder. The woman still refused. End of discussion. No Mike Eruzione birthday present for the daughter of any Yankee-loving sad case of a mother. Sorry, kid.

2. There was a raffle. One of the prizes was an official NFL football that Flutie would sign. Now 41 years old, still active, a backup quarterback with the San Diego Chargers, he was handed the ball and a Sharpie. A young guy, 30 tops, came up to the stage as the winner.

"I'm not going to just hand you the ball," Flutie said, signing his name across the pigskin. "Go long. Take a right at the truck."

The young guy ran a route through the crowd and to the driveway where the truck, maybe 20 feet long, was parked. He went to the end of the truck, took a right, disappeared for a second, then came out the other side. The ball was waiting for him. Standing in street clothes, behind a table, underneath an overhang, everybody watching, Flutie threw a perfect 30-yard spiral, easy and soft, a down-filled pillow dropping from the sky. How good was that? How different are these guys who do this for a living than the rest of us? Flutie was as casual with his motion as if he simply were passing the salt across the table.

The guy dropped the ball.

3. David Ortiz was the star. Maybe it was the fact that the audience had come straight from the win over the Yankees, or maybe it was the fact that the other three athletes were older, that their exploits were further removed in the public mind . . . whatever it was, Ortiz was the star.

The people looked at him differently. You could see them, staring up at the table. The other players, okay, they were interesting. Ortiz had rock star magic. Boston forever has been a baseball town—the crowd at City Hall for the celebration of the New England Patriots' 2002 Super Bowl win chanted "Yankees suck"—but the interest had become amped even further with the dramatics of the 2003 season. (A sports marketing maxim is that the best marketing finish is a close second, the fan returning next year, keyed up for redemption, for the next chapter in the story. If so, the Red Sox have been the most successful marketing franchise in American sports history.) This obviously was that year of redemption. All seats at Fenway, a place with the most expensive tickets in baseball, would be sold out for the season for the first time. The Fox network even had televised the Friday night game nationally in prime time, "The Show-down in Beantown," the first prime-time regular-season broadcast in three years.

All of this love and interest had landed on Ortiz. How about that? I don't think I ever had heard him speak. I did-n't even know if he could speak English. Television shies away from second-language interviews, having no time for the thoughtful, slow reply in a rat-a-tat presentation. It is a disservice to the Latin ballplayers who occupy most of the upper echelon of the game now, and a disservice to the fan, but the practice probably won't be changed soon.

Ortiz, it turned out, spoke quite well. You had to strain a bit to understand him, but if you did—and this was an au-dience more than ready—he made you laugh. Answering a question about whether Manny Ramirez, portrayed often as an airhead, truly came from another world, Ortiz gave a lengthy defense of his teammate. Manny was a great hitter. Manny played hard. Manny worked as much as anyone worked. Ortiz then smiled and added, "To answer the ques-tion, yes, Manny comes from Mars." Answering a question about "what sports event, other than one you played in, re-ally excited you," he said, "The Patriots' win in the Super Bowl last year. I was home in the Dominican. I was in a bar. I was really cheering for the Patriots. I was drunk."

The people laughed. They couldn't get enough of him. Here were three other athletes on the stage who were ac-cepted Boston legends involved in accepted legendary Boston moments. Two were local kids who became famous.

The third, the Houdini of the hardwood, Mr. Basketball, had been around Boston for 50 years. And here was this 28-year-old guy from the Dominican Republic, adopted in a hurry, Big Papi, starting his second local season, and he was the star.

One of the last questions was "What would you like to be if you weren't what you are?" Cousy, no fool, said at his age he'd like to be sitting on a porch somewhere in a rocker, listening to the Red Sox finally beat the Curse of the Bambino (big cheer). Eruzione explained that he already was living a second life, coaching at Boston University. Flutie said he would like to be a coach. The microphone was passed to Ortiz. He said he would like to be a professional basketball player. The microphone was passed to me.

What would I like to be if I wasn't what I am? I put my hand on David Ortiz's shoulder.

"I would like to be him," I said.

I also am no fool.

My nemesis through the years has been Charlie Costanzo. He is one of the neighborhood urchins from the Garden Street Athletic Club in New Haven, now a lawyer in Guilford, Connecticut. He is a Yankees fan from a family of Yankees fans. His father, a sweetheart, a longtime usher at the Yale Bowl who would give us a wink to get into the good seats for football games, was such a Yankees fan that he was buried in a blue, satin Yankees warm-up jacket. This is absolutely true. I was at the wake. Charlie's son,

Chuck-a-Luck, spent some time in Boston after graduating college. He would go to games at Fenway wearing a blue T-shirt that read "Boston Red Sox, World Champions, 1918" on the front. On the back were the words "New York Yankees, World Champions," followed by a list of the team's 26 years of glory. The family always has been sick.

Charlie tortured me throughout high school, college, all of recorded history. Our relationship in this matter developed into one of master and angry servant. He became haughty, privileged. The results every year were no surprise. You, perhaps, had thought something else would happen? Silly you. The Yankees always win. It is a fact of life. I became hesitant, tried to act with caution. Resigned. When the annual con came, the Red Sox starting to show some signs of life, I would hold back and hold back until I could hold back no more. I invariably would make the phone call, blurting out some words to the effect that this was the year, my friend, this was the year. I invariably would pay for this.

"My son and I enjoyed the game," Charlie said after the 2003 Aaron Boone homer. "It was quite exciting. Everyone up there must be feeling pretty sad. I'm sorry for you people."

"I hate you all," I said. "I hate your dead father in his Yankees jacket. I hate your misguided son. I hate you most of all."

I went to the barricades early this year. The Red Sox wound up winning three of four in that first series at Fenway. Then they went to Yankee Stadium the next weekend and swept all three games. A-Rod looked like a bust. Jeter was in the worst slump of his career. The Yankees looked like they had no pitching. The Red Sox were in first in the American League East with a 12–6 record. The Yankees were 8–11 and in third place, floundering. I couldn't control myself.

A few minutes after a bewildered center fielder named Bubba Crosby totally lost a fly ball in the same stretch of grass where Mickey Mantle once roamed, part of an 11–2 Red Sox romp on Friday night in New York, I dialed the phone. The conversation went something like this:

"Are you watching the game?"

"Sure, I'm watching the game."

"I mean, are you really watching the game?"

"It's early in the season."

"Bubba Crosby!"

"Early."

The ante was into the pot. I was on the hook for the entire season. The Red Sox came home to win three straight over Tampa Bay and stretch their record to 15–6. (Unbeatable.) Then they went on the road and lost five in a row in Cleveland and Texas. (Oh my.) The annual ride had begun.

I was running around for most of the summer promoting a biography of Ted Williams—*Ted Williams: The Biography of an American Hero*, Doubleday, $26.95, still available at all bookstores—that had taken me two years to write. Marty Appel, one of a string of former publicity directors for the Yankees hired and fired by George Steinbrenner, was handling the PR. He was another Yankees man I could bait.

"Fans building statue of Mark Bellhorn in Kenmore Square, . . . " I typed in an email.

"Still early," Marty replied. "You guys are always crazy up there."

He booked me for a bunch of weird talk shows around the country by phone. Invariably, the host would move the conversation from Ted to the current situation and the curse and ask for a prediction. I invariably would reply that this was the year, then add that this was what I had been saying for the last 86 years.

In New York, Marty put me on the syndicated *Tim Mc-Carver Show*. McCarver, the Fox baseball analyst and former St. Louis Cardinals catcher, had an observation about baseball in Boston.

"Boston's a different place," he said during a commercial break. "There's no other place like it, the way the people take sides. I go back to the '67 World Series. We came into Boston and were amazed. We'd never played in a place where people hated us. All the cities in the National League, it never was like that. These people hated us. You got that everywhere you went. The cab drivers hated us. The people in the hotel hated us. Everybody hated us.

"And that was in 1967. It's just gotten bigger and bigger ever since. The playoffs last year against the Yankees were unbelievable, the emotion up there. It was just everywhere."

Marty Appel had an addendum to baseball hate. His employment with the Yankees was during the Billy Martin years, when part of the rivalry was a mutual dislike between Red Sox catcher Carlton Fisk and Yankees catcher Thurman Munson.

"There was nothing phony about it on Thurman's side," Marty said. "He just hated Fisk. You could see why, because he was this feisty squat guy and Fisk was big and handsome. Thurman thought everybody favored Fisk.

"One day the Red Sox were in town, and I put out a little pregame collection of stats and notes. Thurman read them and was enraged. I had put in an innocuous note in that Fisk led American League catchers with 16 assists. Thurman was second with 13. He screamed at me that it was a meaningless stat and why would I ever put it in? I told him it was no big deal, but he was still mad.

"The game starts and somebody strikes out. Thurman drops the ball. He stands up, throws to first, turns around, and points a finger to me in the press box. Another guy strikes out. Thurman drops the ball again. Same thing. Points. A third guy strikes out. Same thing. Stares right at me. Okay, Thurman. You're now tied with Carlton Fisk for most assists by a catcher."

By the last weekend in July, alas, it looked like the winners and losers in the rivalry were going to finish in their familiar places. I wasn't calling Charlie. (He was calling me.) I was sticking to business with Marty. (No mention of that Bellhorn statue.) The Red Sox were eight and a half games behind the Yankees, looking bad. (Okay, so it had been early.) The hitting wasn't what it was supposed to be. The fielding was just awful. The Yankees had kicked into fine, efficient form. The Red Sox were gagging.

Marty had scheduled me to sell books at Augur's Book Store in Cooperstown, New York. It was Hall of Fame weekend, the small town packed for the induction of Dennis Eckersley and Paul Molitor. Since Eckersley had made two stops in his career in Boston and lived there now, sometimes working as a postgame analyst, a large number of Red Sox fans walked the streets. Since Cooperstown is in New York, at least as many Yankees fans were in attendance. Everybody seemed to be wearing shirts, hats, gear.

I sat in front of Augur's with five other guys selling and autographing books. Autographs were a sort of currency in the town. Various Hall of Famers and long-ago players were at various shops signing their names for money. The prices started at maybe $35 for the signature of some banjo-hitting utility infielder from the fifties to the $100 per signature that Willie Mays was getting across the street. The other book signers and I were at the lowest end of the scale.

"Here's the deal," I would tell prospective customers. "The autograph is $26.95, cheapest in town. Plus you get the book free."

It was like working at a craft fair.

Somewhere in the afternoon, people started talking about a big fight. The Red Sox were playing the Yankees at Fenway, and Bronson Arroyo had plunked A-Rod . . . and A-Rod had said something . . . and Jason Varitek had stood up and whacked A-Rod in the face . . . and the benches had cleared and there were all kinds of fights! I closed up shop, walked around the corner to the nearest bar, and watched the rest of the game, which ended up being the turnaround for the season.

The bar was full, half Red Sox fans, half Yankees, back and forth, no stopping. Every play was half-groan, half-cheer. The game went on and on, one turn after another, a classic Fenway slugout until Bill Mueller's two-run homer with one out in the ninth. Final cheers. Final groans. My new best friend, a local guy named Charlie Murray, hugged me.

"I've always been a big Red Sox fan," he said. "I grew up in Brockton, Mass. One summer, my dad had to go out to Akron, Ohio, on business, so my brother and I went with him for the ride. On the way back we saw the sign for Cooperstown. My brother said, 'Let's go over and take a look.' None of us ever had been here.

"I was in town for five minutes and decided this was where I was meant to be. I fell in love. Baseball. All this baseball. I went home to my girlfriend and told her I was moving to Cooperstown in two weeks. She could come with me or stay, whatever she wanted to do. I came. She followed a month later. We got married and have been here for ten years. I still love the place. I walk down the street, every day, I feel like I'm ten years old again."

The Nomar trade came a week later. The end of the season unfurled from there, the Red Sox's climb back into contention, the disappointment in New York and then in Boston, Pedro whacked around both times and calling the Yankees "my daddy." Three games out in the end. Wild card. In the playoffs. Good enough. I could use the phone again.

"I'd like to extend my congratulations for first place during the regular season," I said.

"No need," Charlie Costanzo said. "There was never any doubt. This was the way it always had been. Everybody knew what would happen."

"We'll see what happens this time in the playoffs," I said. "I hope the Red Sox play you guys."

"Who's your daddy?" Charlie Costanzo asked.

I went to the third playoff game in the first round against the Anaheim Angels. I had been to only two games at Fenway during the season with my wife and two stepchildren, buying tickets in the bleachers for $50 apiece from a scalper for one of them. (Whatever happened to the concept of baseball as a low-budget family sport? Each night out cost over $300.) The Angels tickets surfaced late from a woman who works for the Baltimore Orioles. The team's owner, Peter Angelos, decided at the last moment that he didn't want to travel to Boston. Two tickets. First-base line. Section 16. Thank you very much.

I went with my married daughter. She was the one of my two kids who fell hardest for the Red Sox and baseball, and we used to go to a bunch of games. She snuck into the 1999 All-Star Game with me, no details available on how we did it, and still was shaking in the sixth inning from the experience. Mark Linchan was compassionate. "I know how you feel," he said. "I felt exactly the same way when I snuck in the first time. Except I was ten years old." The Angels game was the first of many visits to the wayback machine in the next three weeks.

"Remember that awful bag you gave me to take to kindergarten?" she asked. "It came from some prizefight. It was kind of white plastic with drawings of boxers on it?"

"Ken Norton and Muhammad Ali," I said. "I remember it well."

"I was the only kid in kindergarten with a Ken Norton, Muhammad Ali book bag. Everybody else had Barney or the Cabbage Patch kids or somebody. I still don't think the scars have healed."

We settled into our new little neighborhood. An over-bearing dad and his too-loud kid sat behind us. The kid continually was yelling bright comments like, "Swing, bat-ter—batter, swing." The dad was continually encouraging him, beaming as if the kid was a sure bet for Harvard. To the right of us were an older woman and her grown son. He was wearing an official Red Sox jacket, just like the one Terry Francona wore, and was intent on scoring the game in a fat scorebook filled with other games he had scored. This obviously was serious business. In front of us was a single man who seemed to switch to lucky positions in times of stress.

For six innings all went well in the neighborhood. Bron-son Arroyo, Mr. Cornrows, cruised on the mound with his high leg kick and slingshot cleverness. The Red Sox picked up runs in the third, fourth, and fifth innings to take a tidy 6–1 lead into the seventh. All the pieces were in place for a nice celebration, a sweep of the best-of-five series.

Then I misspoke. I forget sometimes that I have the ability to influence games. I was reminded in a hurry.

"You like a 6–1 lead, don't you?" I said to my daughter. "For you a good game is a game where the Red Sox deliver a merciless beating. Am I right?"

"Sure," she replied. "And I know what you're going to say next. Don't say it."

"I like a close game," I said nevertheless. "I want the thrills. I want the memorable. The seat-squirmer."

"Dad . . ."

Before a man could say "Vladimir Guerrero," the Angels star had absolutely pounded a grand-slam homer off reliever Mike Timlin straight on a line into the bleachers. Another Angels run had tied the score. My daughter wouldn't speak to me. A quiet descended over Fenway Park.

This was the sound, the nonsound, of communal fretting. Total worry. I don't think it's heard (not heard?) in any other ballpark in the land. The load of the 86 years, the past disappointments, surfaced this fast. How close had it been to the skin to arrive so quickly? Touch a Red Sox fan and the bruise emerges. It was as if 35,000 people now were gathered to await the results of a biopsy. No good could be imagined. The overbearing father in back did say something bad and loud about the wisdom of bringing Timlin into the game, and the Terry Francona jacket did take offense, and the two of them did seem headed for a tango ("You don't know what you're talking about!" Overbearing Father shouted. "I played college baseball!" Francona Jacket shouted in return), but they eventually returned their attention to the action.

The quiet stretched across the next two innings and then into the uncharted territory of extra innings. My daughter glared at me. My good friend David Ortiz, the man I'd like to be if I weren't me, came to the rescue.

In the bottom of the tenth, two outs, runner on second, Jarrod Washburn brought in to pitch, Ortiz tagged a hanging slider, the first pitch Washburn threw, and sent it in an opposite-field parabola into the seats on top of the Green Monster. Silence was replaced by pandemonium, worry by high-five joy.

A stage was pulled out from under the center-field bleachers. The Dropkick Murphys began to play that Tessie song.

"I told you the close games are better," I told my daughter. "Isn't your dad right again?"

No answer. Bring on the Yankees.

Eight nights later in October 2004, the telephone rang sometime after midnight. Normally this would be a moment of great concern. Who's sick? What happened? Who would be calling this late at night? There was no great concern here.

"Hello, Charlie," I answered.

"Who's your daddy?" Charlie Costanzo asked.

There will be people in the future—there are people now, in fact—who will tell you that they knew exactly what was going to happen next for the Boston Red Sox. They will say they had "a feeling" that everything was going to turn out right and joyous. I don't believe one of them.

The night of October 16, 2004, was a classic low point in angst history. Looking back at it now, I can see it was a final cathartic shudder, one last visit to the graveyard of broken dreams, broken promises, broken-bat singles that always seemed to bloop over the shortstop's head into center field. Looked at then, it was the pits. The Yankees not only were ahead, 3–0, in the ALCS, just about ruling out this latest edition of "Okay, well, this is our year," but that third win was by a 19–8 score at Fenway. The levels of indignity and embarrassment went through the roof. This was supposed to be the team that was built for a championship run? In the last year of all those free-agent contracts, the money team, not as rich as the Yankees but richer than anyone else, this was the best these guys could do? The optimism of four days earlier—heck, four hours earlier—seemed laughable. Check us out. We're the ones with the custard pie on our faces. That's seltzer water mixing with our tears.

I watched game four almost out of obligation. There was a little bit of that "Win one, just be respectable," but not a lot. The two worst things that could have happened to the Red Sox had happened. Schilling was hurt with his ankle tendon deal. The Red Sox bats had gone quiet. Figured. Just figured.

By the ninth inning, not much had changed. The Yankees were ahead, 4–3, three outs away from the sweep, and Mariano Rivera was on the mound. Looking at Rivera was like looking across the desk at the loan officer at the downtown savings bank with no collateral in your pocket. No, no, no. The guy never smiles. He just gets people out, one-two-three, and goes home for dinner.

Except this time, Kevin Millar walked . . .

And Dave Roberts ran for him . . .

And stole second base.

The Red Sox had a runner on second base in the ninth inning without a hit with no men out. This was an event noteworthy in club history. Other teams did this for 86 years against the Red Sox. Other teams killed the Red Sox with this. The slow, plodding, never-steal-a-base Red Sox never did this. Never. Now they did.

When Bill Mueller singled home Roberts to tie the game, the earth somehow tilted on its axis. A cosmic change occurred. Nothing bad would ever happen again. The most un–Red Sox run in Red Sox history had changed history. Except no one knew it.

When my good friend, the man who I would be if I wasn't me, Big Papi, pounded his walk-off home run in the 12th for a 6–4 win, the ball of success was rolling. There wasn't cause to run out on the street and wake the neighbors, but the moment felt very good and the mind started clicking. Lets' see, Pedro pitches tomorrow night. Then Schilling pitches game six in New York, and game seven, take your chances. Derek Lowe has been pretty good. There was a reason Las Vegas had favored the Red Sox before the Series began, and that reason was pitching. The Red Sox's pitching now was lined up quite nicely.

I went to the game the next night with Mark Linehan and Ian Thomsen. We stood in back and for ten bucks apiece had our pictures taken with Nelson de LaRosa, the incredibly tiny midget from the Dominican Republic who is friends with Pedro Martinez. We left in the eighth inning to watch the end of the game at the Baseball Tavern. Once again, the action went into extra innings. Fourteen innings. The man who I would be if I wasn't me won it, 5–4, with a bloop single, another uncharacteristic Red Sox event. There was great celebration at the Tavern. There was beer. I came home with a smile on my face and a Polaroid picture of myself with a midget.

"Quite a game," I told my wife.

"Quite a game," MaryEllen Montville agreed.

She and I watched the next two games at home. The cosmic change was obvious. The Red Sox were at the Stadium, where bad things always happened, but they wouldn't happen now. The Red Sox had their pitching in order this time, Schilling with his magic sutures for game six, the rejuvenated Derek Lowe for game seven. The Red Sox were getting the calls on the weird plays—A-Rod slapping the ball, the safe-out call at third. The Red Sox were winning, 4–2, in game six, 10–3 in game seven. They did something that no team ever had done, coming back from a 0–3 deficit. They did it against the Yankees, the first time they had beaten the Yankees in a meaningful situation in a hundred years. If you listened closely you could hear the trumpets. Or maybe those were the sirens for the out-of-control college kids, celebrating in Kenmore Square.

I didn't call Charlie Costanzo at the moment. I waited until the next day. I tried to act with dignity. He responded in kind. He said the Red Sox were just better. He said he was surprised how empty he felt. I told him I knew the feeling. He said friends, Yankees fans, had been calling all day. They all said they didn't know what to do. I told him I didn't know what to do.

"I'm not watching the World Series," Costanzo said. "I made my own little protest. I bought a copy of *Street and Smith's Annual* today. I am officially devoting myself to college basketball."

I said that I, in fact, probably was going to watch the World Series.

❖

The Series turned out to be a four-game anticlimax. Was it not? A parade. The St. Louis Cardinals never appeared. Where was all that inside-baseball stuff they were supposed to use? Where was all the power? The drama was all contained in the Yankees series. That was the purge, the hurdle. The World Series was the formality, the beginning of the celebration.

I watched the final game at home with my wife. We had visitors, my sister-in-law Kathy, and her friend Carmel from Ireland and Carmel's daughter Amy. Carmel and Amy knew nothing about baseball and the Red Sox, and I explained it all. They were shaky about the significance.

"Eight-six years is it?"

"Never won?"

"Isn't that a long time?"

When the game ended, final out, we opened a bottle of champagne. I kissed my wife. I high-fived my sister-in-law and the Irish people. MaryEllen's daughter Ashley called from prep school, dormitory excitement in the background. I called my daughter and her husband. She said she cried at the end. I called my son in New York. He said he had cried. We drank champagne and watched the muted celebrations around the city.

Two nights later I tried to put my feelings into words. I wrote a column for the *Globe*'s fat souvenir section that would appear in the Sunday paper. It was an honor. Sports editor Joe Sullivan said the section had grown so large with the excitement that the *Globe* had sold over a million dollars' worth of ads.

The words were these:

MY STORY (CODA)

I learned how to fly a few minutes before midnight on Oct. 27, 2004. I always thought I could fly, watching those seagulls gracefully drop out of the sky to spear yet another French fry from the MDC trash cans across from Kelly's Roast Beef in Revere, but I never had given it a shot. The Boston Red Sox gave me strength.

"If the Red Sox can win the World Series," I said, stepping from the house just moments after reliever Keith Foulke fielded a ground ball and flipped it to first baseman Doug Mientkiewicz for the final out and the 4–0 sweep over the St. Louis Cardinals, "then I surely can fly."

I flapped my arms as fast I could, jumped into the air and was off. Simple as that. I soon was soaring across the Boston harbor and then downtown and then directly over the celebrating crowds in Kenmore Square. I buzzed a couple of Northeastern University kids climbing a lamppost, startled a TPF trooper into dropping his truncheon, took a hard left at the Prudential Building and glided back home.

"I can fly!" I exclaimed to my cocker spaniel, Slugger, the only one still awake in the house.

"Sacre bleu!" he replied.

I always thought Slugger could talk. He would stare at me with those brown eyes and that little panting sound and I knew conversation was possible. Now he could. In French. And I could understand him. I always thought I could understand French, three years in high school, just wishing the people would slow down when they talked, and now I had no problem.

179

"Tres bien, beau chien," I said.

I slept my best sleep in ages—a delightful dream in the middle involving New York Yankees owner George Steinbrenner, chained to a post in the lowest circle of hell—and made breakfast for the family in the morning. I always knew I could make perfect Eggs Benedict. I sang while I served, exactly like Frank Sinatra. I moved exactly like Fred Astaire. I always knew I could tap dance.

I felt an energy I hadn't felt in years. I felt as strong as David Ortiz. I felt as fast as Dave Roberts, as happy as Manny Ramirez, as focused as Curt Schilling, as solid as Jason Varitek, as smart as Theo Epstein. I whistled "Sweet Caroline" (uh-uh-ohh), typed out a 500-page novel that I always knew I had inside me, took care of some plumbing and electrical work around the house that I always knew I could do if I just tried, yodeled good-bye (I always knew I could yodel) and hit the streets.

What next? I ran from Hopkinton to Boston, just for the heck of it. I walked on my hands. I juggled a Ted Williams baseball card, a copy of the *Baseball Encyclopedia* and an apple. Didn't drop a one. I swam with the L Street Brownies. I dunked a basketball. Backwards. After jumping over a Toyota. I drove the length of Massachusetts Avenue and all the lights were green. Every one of them.

I found a parking space. I found an honest politician. I tried broccoli and liked it. Every now and then a picture would pop into my head. Ortiz, clapping his two hands,

grabbing the bat, swinging as hard as he could, the baseball flying into the night. Schilling, the dollop of blood
on his white sock. Derek Jeter looking befuddled. Every
office I called, a real person answered the phone. I signed
to appear in a feature film. (Leading man.) I was computer literate. I baked a cake. I changed my own oil. Fast
as a cat, I multiplied large numbers in my head.

All items were on sale everywhere. All stocks were up.
The pictures just kept coming. All those people that the
Fox network showed biting their nails, crossing their fingers and their toes during the first three games against
the Yankees. Where were they now? What were they
doing? Derek Lowe on the mound. Talking to himself.
Mark Bellhorn. Saying nothing. I played the piano, dis-
covered I had a strong left hand. Went to the post office
and found no lines. Rollerbladed. Rode a motorcycle.
Never fell down. I always knew I could that. I booked a
trip to the Dominican Republic. I joined a gym, started a
diet, bought a new suit of clothes. Something funky.

The Charles River—it appeared to me, at least—had
been turned into buttermilk. The John Hancock building
now was made out of chocolate. The strings on the
Zakim Bridge played a melody when the wind hit them
just right. The hospitals all were empty. The churches all
were full. A heart seemed to beat in the middle of Fenway Park, right under the pitcher's mound.

I always had wondered what it would be like when the
Red Sox won the Series. I suppose everyone under the
age of 86 in New England had wondered. The Red Sox
story had gone along for so many years with its annual

disappointments that the pain had become an almost masochistic delight. Sort of like record snowstorms in winter. Sort of like the daily bad cup of coffee from the company cafeteria. Sort of like a mole on the tip of your nose. Endurance and acceptance had become virtues. Life had to be lived within limitations.

What would it be like without those limitations?

I suppose I'm not much different from anyone else around here. I thought about departed friends and long-ago moments. I heard from people I hadn't heard from in years. I told my wife I loved her. I told my kids I loved them. I drank a little champagne. I flew through the air. I talked to my dog in French and he talked back. I smiled a lot.

I say so far so good.

I finished after midnight and sent the column to the *Globe* sports desk. Ken Fratus, one of the editors, asked if I had known what he and copy editor Bob Fedus had done. I told him I didn't. He said that they already had checked off one of the things in the column. They had vowed to swim at L Street if the Red Sox ever won the Series, and they already had done it. I asked him how the water felt.

"Not as cold as you'd think," he said.

Lovely.

I had an impulse to call Charlie Costanzo, to wake him up, ask him what teams are going to be strong this year in the Big Sky conference, but I let it pass. I went to bed. I had a parade to attend in the morning.

Acknowledgments

THANKS TO EVERYONE I INTERVIEWED FOR THIS BOOK. Special thanks to Sean Kelly and Eric Christensen of the Sons of Sam Horn, to Glen Geffner of the Boston Red Sox and to Mark Linehan and to Paul Doyle for their contributions. Thanks to Esther Newberg for getting the ball rolling and to Kate Darnton, Peter Osnos, Gene Taft, David Patterson, and the people at PublicAffairs, for keeping it rolling to the end. Thanks always on the home front to my wife Samantha and to Alex and Ashley and to my children, Leigh and Robin, and Robin's husband, Doug.

Thanks, too, to the 2004 Boston Red Sox for the ride.